Furnishing the World

Phillip Barnett's Shop, 96 Curtain Road, EC2 1910
Rosalind Bradley discovered this photograph of her grandfather's shop whilst
researching her family history.
(London Borough of Hackney Archives Department)

FURNISHING THE WORLD

THE EAST LONDON FURNITURE TRADE 1830-1980

by

Pat Kirkham

Rodney Mace

Julia Porter

JOURNEYMAN

First published in Great Britain by the Journeyman Press Limited, 97 Ferme Park Road, Crouch End, London, N8 9SA

This publication has been made possible with the financial support of 'The Friends of the Geffrye Museum', whose aim is to acquaint the public with the Museum, assist its many projects and educational work, and help acquire furniture and works of art to enhance its already important collection. For further information please contact Mrs Z Plews, Hon. Secretary, at the Geffrye Museum, Kingsland Road, London, E2 8EA.

Copyright © by the Geffrye Museum, 1987

British Library Cataloguing in Publication Data

Kirkham, Pat
  Furnishing the world : the East End
  furniture trade 1830-1980.
  1. Furniture industry and trade—England
  —London—History 2. London (England)—
  Industries—History
  I. Title   II. Mace, Rodney   III. Porter,
  Julia
  338.7'6841'0094215   HD9773.G73L6

ISBN 1-85172-008-1

First edition 1987

Designed by the DEGW Partnership, London

Photoset in Futura by Lightning Graphics, London

Printed in Great Britain by Staples Printers Rochester Limited, Love Lane, Rochester, Kent.

ACKNOWLEDGEMENTS

Mr Adams, Ivor Adamson, Mr Alabaster, Alfred Alexander, Ros Allwood, Adrian Amos, Edward Amos, Sue Ashworth, Stephen Astbury, Association of Master Upholsterers, Sophia Baron, Mr Barraclough, Jeffery Baum, Tony Barwick, Frederick Beaken, David Beevers, Mr Billingham, Pam Birley, Bishopsgate Institute, Bill Boosey, Bill Borland, Dee Bourne, Victor Bourne, Rosalind Bradley, David Brown, Henry Bridger-Rye, British Library, British Museum, Rickie Burman, Business Archives Council, Helen Carpenter, Mrs Carron, Annette Carruthers, Bob Carter, Mr Cecil, Ruth Charity, Lesley Charteris, Mr Choules, Colin Christopher, Cintique, Mrs Clark, Helena Cleary, Frank Cohen, John Cole, Andrew Constable, Jeremy Cooper, Bill Cotton, Chris Denvir, Design Council, Henry Doncaster, Mr Eisen, Pierre Elena, Chris Elmers, Mr Epstein, Sian Evans, Sophie de Falbe, Fawcett Library, Honor Flanagan, Mr Flood, Mr and Mrs Foster, Moira Fraser-Steele, Mayerlene Frow, Furniture Industries Research Association Library, Furniture, Timber and Allied Trades Union, Tom Gambles, Mr Gilson, David Ginsberg, Peter Goodman, Mr Gray, Greater London Enterprise Board, Greater London Industrial Archaeology Society, Greater London Photographic Library, Mr Griffiths, Don Grunwell, Hackney Archives Department, Hackney Economic Development Unit, Rosalinda Hardiman, Robin Hartley, Heal's Archive, Rachel Hastead, David Heath, Felicity Hebditch, Philip Henderson, Benjamin Hill, Hille International Ltd., Lesley Hoskins, Alan Hunt, Valerie Hughes, Independent Designers Federation, Islington Archives Department, Mrs Jennings, Mr Jordan, Andy Kindler, Mr Kogan, Simon Lace, James Latham, Kedrun Laurie, Mr Lee, Maxine Leonard, Sissy Lewis, London College of Furniture, London History Workshop, London Strategic Policies Unit, Paul Lucas, Terry McCarthy, Sally Macdonald, Jane Mace, Manchester Studies Centre, Miss Marigold, Victor Mark, Bill Massill, Modern Records Centre (University of Warwick), Morning Star, Jack Moss, Museum of the Jewish East End, Museum of London, Mrs Murray, Rebecca Myram, Tom Nannery, National Art Library, National Film Archive, National Museum of Labour History, Ines Newman, Arthur Norval, Ann Oliver, Ian Oppenheim, John Penfold, Portsmouth Museums, Mr Prior, Robert Pryce, Margaret Roberts, Nathan Rosenberg, Mrs Rowe, RIBA Library, Mr Sambridge, Raphael Samuel, Reginald Sanders, Edward Sanson, Cherrill Scheer, Pam Schweitzer, Science Museum Library, Morris and Rhoda Serlin, Michael Serota, Jock Shanley, Shoreditch Reference Library, Shoreditch Society, Mr Silk, Mr Simon, Silver Studio Collection (Middlesex Polytechnic), Glynn Smith, Clare Storey, Mr Strutt, Mr Sumner, David Thomas, Terry Thorp, Tottenham Jewish Research Group, Tower Hamlets Archives Department, TUC Library, Jack Trainis, Mark Turner, Anthony Vaughan, Vestry House Museum, Victoria & Albert Museum, Mrs Walter, Westminster Libraries, George Wood, Elizabeth Woods, Miss Woods, Doris Young, Hilary Young

The authors are especially grateful to Julia Shelley for her contribution of material on Jewish workers and training.

CONTENTS

The Geffrye Museum: Exterior 1987
(Inner London Education Authority)

The Geffrye Museum: Woodworker's Shop 1975
(Inner London Education Authority)

PREFACE

For 150 years, east London has pioneered developments in furniture making in Britain. One of the great industries of the East End, it was at its height in 1914 when the London County Council established a museum of furniture and woodworking in the old Geffrye Almshouses, Shoreditch, then at the heart of the trade. The Geffrye Museum is now famous for its collection of English domestic furniture and woodwork, which has been displayed in a series of period rooms since the 1930s, when the museum came under the LCC Education Committee, now the Inner London Education Authority.

In recent years the museum has started to document the industry on its doorsteps by collecting tools, trade catalogues, photographs, trade ephemera, furniture designs, people's memories, and if space permits, the furniture itself. Two booklets have already been published by the ILEA — *Sam: An East End Cabinet Maker* (1983) and *The Vaughans: East End Furniture Makers* (1985). Drawing together recent research and incorporating new material from oral history interviews, this book, which has been written to accompany a major exhibition at the museum in 1978 (July 3 -January 3), begins to construct a clear picture of the context in which the furniture was made. Part 1 introduces the crafts of furniture making and traces the rise and fall of the industry from around 1830 to today. The organisation of distribution and marketing was separate from manufacturing. This is described in Part 2. Trade union organisation has been important in improving working practices and conditions. Part 3 gives an account of unionisation in east London and discusses some of the central issues in each period. In order to give some sense of the different jobs that people did and their daily lives, Part 4 contains edited interviews with men and women who have worked in the trade, which cover a period from 1850 to the present. Although this book is chiefly concerned with the east London trade, it illuminates at the same time aspects of furniture making in general.

Little has been written about the history of the furniture trade in Britain. Furniture historians have until recently been mainly interested in pieces made by known designers, not with the social and economic context in which they were produced. East End furniture has been dismissed as vulgar, mass-produced, 'commercial debasement'. One of the delights of this project has been the discovery that every kind of furniture imaginable has been produced in the workshops and factories of east London and that it reached all kinds of homes throughout Britain and all over the world. London was the centre of the furniture trade and by the 1880s most of the trade was concentrated in the East End. When the London Cabinet Trades Federation adopted the motto 'London Furnishes the World' in the early part of this century, it was in fact east London that was 'furnishing the world'.

The main purpose of this book, and the accompanying exhibition, is to show how the furniture used in ordinary homes was made and to reveal something of the social conditions in which it was produced. The Geffrye Museum has chosen 1987 to celebrate 150 years of furniture making in east London. This book is written for all those who have worked, and those who still work, in the local furniture industry.

The Geffrye Museum: Early Georgian Room 1949
The painted figures and scenes through the windows can no longer be seen. Recent reorganisation has involved the rearrangement of the panelling and the inclusion of a reproduction floor cloth.
(Leonard Taylor)

Cabinet maker's tool chest
(Old woodworking tools)

Chapter One

FURNITURE MAKING:
The Rise and Fall of an East London Industry

Garret master hawking chest of drawers 1860
This classic picture was first reproduced in Henry Mayhew's **London Labour**
and the London Poor, vol.3 1861.
(Photo Studios)

FURNITURE MAKING:
The Rise and Fall of an East London Industry

Furniture making began in London's East End in the first half of the nineteenth century. It grew rapidly from the 1840s and became one of the main occupations of that area, the others being tailoring and boot and shoe making. By 1870 the East End outstripped the West End as the main furniture producing area in the capital.

Although furniture making developed relatively late in East London, the capital itself had been a centre of furniture production from the Middle Ages. By the seventeenth and eighteenth centuries, furniture making was a thriving trade in London which led the nation in fashionable taste. London was the seat of government and it housed the royal court. The rich and influential spent part of every year there and ordered much of the furniture for their country homes as well as most of the furniture for their houses in the capital itself. The river Thames gave merchants access to imported timber, the port's largest import in terms of bulk. Furthermore, by the eighteenth century, London was the world's leading financial and commercial centre which made it ideally placed for an expanding export trade and brought rich rewards for the growing merchant class. The latter also demanded quality furniture and furnishings.

Although furniture made in London was sold throughout the United Kingdom and all over the world, her own expanding population in itself provided an enormous market. The metropolitan population grew rapidly; from about 575,000 in 1700 to about 675,000 in 1750, reaching over 900,000 by 1801 when it accounted for nearly one-tenth of the total population of England and Wales. By 1840 it was about 2,225,000 and by 1911 it stood at 7,250,000, making it the largest single market for manufactured goods in the country. Furniture making was always highly concentrated in London. From the mid-nineteenth to the mid-twentieth century just under two-fifths of all furniture makers in England and Wales worked in the capital.

Until the mid-nineteenth century the quality firms of the West End and City produced most of the furniture made in London but from about 1840 there came an ever increasing demand for furniture of less high qual-

ity. This was partly in response to the population growth which, in turn, led to re-development and new housing. As Henry Mayhew noted in *The Morning Chronicle* in 1850:

Since 1839 there have been 200 miles of new streets formed in London, no less than 6,405 new dwellings have been erected annually since that time; and, it is but fair to assume that the majority of these new homes must have required new furniture.

These homes were for 'middle' and 'lower middle' class people and also for respectable artisans who wanted furniture similar in appearance to but cheaper than that bought by the wealthier sections of the community. It was upon this market that the East End trade was based and it gradually extended out to provide furniture for every social class.

In the nineteenth century the West and East sections of the furniture trade roughly coincided with what were known as the 'honourable' and 'dishonourable' (or 'slop') sectors of the trade. The West End mainly produced high quality goods with highly skilled labour trained through an apprenticeship system. There was little division of labour: the 'all round' craft workers made pieces of furniture from start to finish. This is not to say that no quality work was made in East London — it was and still is. Nevertheless, the mainstay of that trade was the cheaper furniture that went into the homes of ordinary working class people and the 'middling' type that made its way into many middle class houses. The East End trade was characterised by small workshops established with very little capital investment, low wages, long hours, the collapse of the apprenticeship system, unskilled labour, sub-contracting, specialisation, the subdivision of labour and a low degree of trade union organisation. Like tailoring and boot making, furniture making was a classic 'sweated trade'.

All aspects of the trade were undertaken, including cabinet making, fancy cabinet making, chair making, carving, gilding and upholstery — whilst a host of allied trades from timber merchants to glue makers and from japanners to brass dealers supplied the furniture makers. These crafts were often undertaken separately one from the other — unlike in the West End where they were normally all gathered together within one large manufactory. In the East End there emerged the sub-contractor — the 'warehouseman', 'middle-man' or 'slaughter-house man', as such people were known — to co-ordinate all the different aspects of production. They bought in frames and carcases from cabinet makers and chair makers and kept them until they had orders before sending them out to carvers, upholsterers, polishers or finishers.

Although furniture making was, and is, a male dominated industry, some women did work in it. In the nineteenth century in the East End they were mainly concentrated in upholstery but in the late nineteenth and twentieth century they also worked as french polishers. Women's lower wages were seen as a threat by most men in a highly cut-throat world. So too was the entrance into the trade of Jewish workers, fleeing persecution in Poland and Russia, who came to London in large numbers between 1881-6, bringing a new cultural dimension to life in the East End. These workers, known as 'greeners', were sometimes blamed for the intense competition obtaining in the East End trade at that time. It was made extremely clear, however, by Gentile and Jewish furniture makers alike in their evidence to a Parliamentary Enquiry on the sweating system in 1888 that the causes lay elsewhere. They argued that it was the subdivision of jobs previously done by a skilled worker and the sub-contracting out of work, either directly or through middlemen, by the large West End retail shops that was the root of all the problems.

> The cheaper market for furniture broadened enormously in the inter-war years when there was a huge increase in the number of new houses built for lower middle class and upper working class families. New materials such as plywood came into use and the larger firms began to mechanise production. New types of furniture, such as the three piece suite and the 'fireside chair', made their appearance and some firms began to specialise in either bedroom suites or dining-room suites. These became available to the poorer sections of the community with the widespread increase in hire purchase arrangements in the inter-war years. The great demand for cheap furniture encouraged expansion and mechanisation with the result that some sizeable firms developed in the East End. However, this very growth in size meant that the biggest firms looked beyond the East End to the Lea Valley where cheap undeveloped land offered the possibility of large factory sites with good communications out of London to provincial markets. Firms such as Lebus had moved out of the old East End before the inter-war years but the main shift towards Tottenham,

Enfield, Edmonton, and Walthamstow came in the late 1930s and after World War II.

In response to these developments, the East End trade specialised increasingly in quality reproduction and contract work in the years following the second World War. It was no longer concerned with the very cheapest furniture because it could not compete with the big outer London firms. Skilled workers became more highly regarded in the trade which managed to tick over until the 1960s when the furniture trade as a whole began to decline. The very severe crisis in the trade since 1979 has resulted in firm after firm closing up and down the country and East London has been no exception. The trade has virtually collapsed, although there are a few glimmers of hope on the horizon which will be discussed at the end of this chapter. Nevertheless, what is left of furniture making in the East End is only a shadow of what was one of London's most thriving and important manufacturing industries.

The Crafts and Division of Labour

One of the main characteristics of the East End furniture trade was an acute division of labour. This meant that untrained, unskilled and cheap labour, usually boys, called 'learners' could be used in the place of the all round skilled craftworker. Before recounting the story of the development of the East End trade, each of the crafts will be examined in order to establish just how far the process of specialisation had gone by that date.

Cabinet making

The cabinet maker was the main woodworking furniture maker and, with the exception of the carver, the most skilled. The range of products made was wide and included carcase furniture such as cabinets, chests-of-drawers, sideboards, wardrobes and bookcases, as well as tables. One of the main features of the craft in the East End was its division into many small tasks requiring little skill or ingenuity. According to Henry Mayhew, a journalist who interviewed furniture makers in the 'dishonourable' sector in 1850, the subdivisions were 'as numerous as the articles of the cabinet maker's calling'. Some cabinet makers made nothing but tables; table making itself came to be subdivided and some workers produced only table legs while others made the rest of the table. Specialisation also took place with reference to different types of tables, particularly games tables such as backgammon tables.

When the cabinet maker Henry Price worked at Hoxton in 1858 he made nothing but wardrobes. At another shop he only made drawers for chests-of-drawers. This particular specialisation was so well established in the East End by the mid-nineteenth century that some men had been trained only in drawer making. This extraordinary degree of subdivision continued right up until the Second World War — and beyond in the case of certain firms. This is not to say that there were no skilled cabinet makers capable of making entire pieces from beginning to end as well as a wide range of products but rather that they were not employed so to do.

New specialisations arose in the East End trade as new products came into vogue. One of the major new furniture types of the inter-war years was the china cabinet, the pride and joy of every working class and lower middle class 'best room'. There were over 120 different designs for china cabinets regularly made up in the East End shops. Some of the less skilled and less patient craftworkers loved working at china cabinets because, since there were no drawers in them, it was not necessary to make dovetail joints. Certain cabinet makers began to specialise in door barring, that is the making of the mouldings that went between the panes of glass in china cabinets. Those who worked at this recall plenty of work, with advertisements not just asking for cabinet makers but for door barrers. Some of these men worked on their own: 'chaps would set up with two benches and a glue pot, sheets of ply for the backing and you were away ...' But many also worked for the small to middling sized firms which made china cabinets their speciality. Coffee tables were also popular in the inter-war years. One man, Dick Hubberly, set up his own firm, Atlas Rims, which specialised in supplying the trade with rims — but only coffee table rims.

Fancy cabinet making

Fancy cabinet making was as separate and distinct from cabinet making as was carving or turning. It covered a host of small, light and portable items of furniture, most of which had some novelty value and were made in decorative or highly figured wood, mainly veneers. A great deal was made for and used by women; indeed, the word 'ladies' was pre-fixed to a variety of pieces such as jewel boxes, dressing cases, work tables, work boxes, portable desks and writing tables. Other small items included chess and backgammon boards, tea chests and tea caddies as well as card, glove, knife, gun and pistol cases.

The introduction of steam powered veneer cutting machinery about 1826 led to a dramatic reduction in the price of veneers which were not only cut more quickly but also more thinly. This in turn, led to a big expansion of fancy cabinet making in the East End, as one who worked in the trade explained:

...machinery has been a benefit to us: it increases the material for our work. If there wasn't so much veneering there wouldn't be so much fancy cabinet work.

The pressure to produce ever cheaper 'cheap luxuries' such as jewel boxes or dressing cases led to subdivisions within fancy cabinet making. The main division was between dressing case making, on the one hand, and desk making, on the other. Even with desk making, however, some men worked only on portable desks.

Although fancy cabinet making involved veneering, the demand for desks and writing boxes in solid wood, particularly walnut, increased in the 1840s. The work was more skilled since veneers could not be used to cover up bad workmanship. Few people could work as well or as quickly at one type as they could at the other and something of a split developed between the fancy cabinet makers who worked in solid wood and those who used veneers. Furthermore, the interiors of work boxes were made by another group of people known as pine workers while the compartments to go inside dressing cases were made by workers known as fitters-up (even though they also worked in pine). Once the interiors were fitted out, they were lined with paper, silk, satin or velvet. This work was done by yet another group, this time by women, usually the wives of fancy cabinet makers. The work was skilful and needed to be done with considerable care but, such was the sexual division of labour, that the part which required 'greater care and nicety', such as the lining of jewel cases with velvets, was usually given over to men.

The demand for small boxes diminished in the twentieth century but a variety of types of small desks continued to be made throughout East London with labour divided in a similar fashion to earlier years.

Chair making

Chairs were amongst the first items of furniture to be made in the East End. From about 1790 to 1803 Stubbs's Chair Manufactory in City Road and Brick Lane produced Gothic and Windsor chairs in yew together with dyed and stained chairs, garden furniture and wheelchairs for invalids. Other chair manufacturers grew up as the East End trade developed, with firms often specialising in one or two types of chairs. In the second half of the nineteenth century many chairmakers made complete chairs from start to finish but, when large numbers of similar chairs were made, some workers were kept at the repetitive task of making only legs, or arms. Such work was usually done by trainee workers or by unskilled labour. Those small chairmakers who had to compete with the larger chair manufacturers also sub-divided up the different aspects of chairmaking and usually employed young boys to do it in order to keep down the costs.

This division of labour continued into the twentieth century, right down to today. One furniture maker working about 1930 recalls that 'there were many people who did precise things and no more'. He had in mind people such as Mr. Webb, a leg shaper who made 'eight cabriole legs in mahogany, with a nicely carved acanthus leaf on the knee, all put into a sack for me to carry away to complete a reproduction desk'.

Upholstery

Upholstery was often referred to as the 'soft' side of the furniture trade and was considered somewhat genteel and refined (as compared to the woodworking crafts) because it was carried out in dust free conditions and workers could wear clean and decent clothes to work. A great deal of upholstery was concerned with seat furniture. As early as 1791 John Allen of Shoreditch was recorded as a chair stuffer, indicating that there was some division of labour in the East End between those who stuffed and those who covered seat furniture. This division increased rapidly as the cheap upholstery trade developed, partly in response to the increased demand in general and partly in response to the fashion for amply upholstered furniture from the 1830s, and by mid-century trainee upholsterers were only taught one or other of these aspects of the craft.

Both men and women worked as chair stuffers in the mid-nineteenth century but there was a degree of division according to gender. The cutting and covering of better quality items was always left to men. When Henry Mayhew reported on the working conditions of upholsteresses in 1849, he noted that they only cut out the cheaper chintz or holland cases which protected furniture stuffed and covered by male workers. However, women and men both undertook sewing, making up curtains, cases and bed furniture as well as joining together carpet pieces.

Although upholstresses were classified as unskilled because they had not undergone any formal training, sewing was traditionally taught to young girls in the home and many achieved very high levels of expertise. Upholstery was cleaner work than other aspects

Cabinet making: workshops, Long Street, E2 1955
(Greater London Photographs Library)

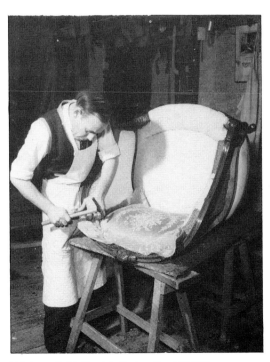

Upholstery: H. & L. Epstein's, Hanbury Street, E1 1955
(Ronald Chapman)

Chair making: H. & L. Epstein's, Hanbury Street, E1 1955
(Ronald Chapman)

Turning: Workshops, Columbia Road, E2 1986
(David Dilley)

of furniture-making and because it was associated with the 'feminine' skill of sewing it was considered sufficiently genteel to be undertaken by women who were 'sober and steady' and of respectable appearance. Henry Mayhew reported that 'there are more old maids employed in the upholstery business than any other'. Many were middle aged and some were the widows of upholsterers but they had one thing in common — they were dependent upon their own wages for their livelihood. The low wages of the East End made that a pitiful livelihood for many of them.

Upholstery continued to be divided into stuffing and covering in the twentieth century. Webbing and springing were often put out to specialists, particularly from the late 1920s onwards when technological developments proceeded rapidly. In the 1930s it was a not uncommon sight in and around Curtain Road to see the frames of three piece suites stacked up outside upholsterers shops 'waiting transit to a neighbour for webbing and springing, and then perhaps a further move to be stuffed and finally covered.'

Turning

After steam powered lathes were introduced in the London furniture trade about 1825, the productivity of the turner doubled, but no new division of labour appeared throughout the nineteenth or in the twentieth century. Those who worked in shops based on cabinet making, or who worked for a middleman supplying general furniture shops, turned table legs, cabinet legs, bed pillars and other items to patterns supplied to them; those who worked for chair makers undertook much more repetitive work, mainly the turning of hundreds and hundreds of chair legs.

Carving

Carving was the most skilled of all the wood working crafts. In nineteenth century London the most skilful exponents worked in the West End trade. Some skilled men worked as carvers in the East End but such were the pressures of competition that, by and large, high quality carving, which inevitably involved considerable labour costs, went by the board. Much of the carving on East End furniture in the nineteenth century, therefore, was 'scamped' and rushed. A great deal of it was eventually replaced by roughly stamped out ornament which was easily and cheaply finished off by a young boy 'learner'.

In the mid-nineteenth century Henry Mayhew noted

about 200-300 carvers working in the Bethnal Green, Curtain Road and Moorfields area. Some of them undertook all aspects of carving associated with furniture making but, for the most part, they specialised. With the exception of those who carved cornices and pillars for beds, furniture carvers divided into two main categories — the chair carvers and cabinet carvers. The latter included those who carved frames and overmantels, a booming aspect of the East End trade, particularly in the second half of the century.

There were several attempts at perfecting machines for carving from the 1840s but they needed to be used regularly and extensively before they were economical. Even then they only roughed out the carving which still had to be finished off by hand. Techniques of burning into wood with templates to produce an effect of old carving had a certain vogue in the middle of the nineteenth century. By and large, however, East End carvers worked by hand or their work was replaced by moulded ornamental substitutes bought in cheaply from specialist suppliers.

French polishing

French polish, a shellac and spirit-based polish which gave a smooth glass-like finish to wood, came into use in the early nineteenth century. The French practitioners of this new method of polishing settled amongst compatriot Spitalfields weavers but found work in both the West End and East End of London. In France it had not constituted a separate craft, but in London it was immediately established as an occupation separate and distinct from other furniture making tasks. A certain division of labour based on gender developed in the late nineteenth and early twentieth century as increasing numbers of women worked as french polishers. The 1881 census recorded 248 female french polishers working in London's East End, mostly on small fancy cabinet work. Although there was no difference in the actual craft process done by female and male polishers and they both had to use the same amount of 'elbow grease' when polishing, women generally tended to work on the smaller items while the very largest pieces of furniture were reserved for men to polish, the implication being that they had greater stamina.

The inter-war years saw great changes in this craft, not directly from the division of labour but from the introduction of quick-drying cellulose lacquers with hard finishes and mechanically operated spray guns. Many East End polishers found themselves made redundant. The new work was done by people who were simply known as sprayers. Many of these were women, including Sissy Lewis whose testimony appears in the final chapter of this book.

All these many subdivisions in the East End trade were geared to producing furniture more quickly and more cheaply than ever before. It took less time and less ability to learn only part of a craft that had once required a seven year apprenticeship to learn in its entirety. The East End was never based on the traditional apprenticeship system, as had been the West End trade (but even that had broken down in the first half of the nineteenth century). Boys may have been referred to as apprentices but they were more often 'learners' taken on for two to four years. They were paid a small wage and, whilst conditions varied from employer to employer and from craft to craft, these young boys were mainly used as cheap labour once they had learned one or two basic aspects of the job. This was what the East End trade was built upon. Employers (large and small) liked to keep employees at one small job because they were less inclined to move to jobs which involved other aspects of furniture making if their 'hand was out'. After months and months of making table legs, for instance, it was difficult for a cabinet maker to change and work with sufficient speed to ensure decent earnings at, say, overmantels, or hanging bookcases.

Carving: H. & L. Epstein's, Hanbury Street, E1 1955
(Ronald Chapman)

Furniture Making comes to East London

There was very little furniture making in the East End before the 1830s and 40s. The main eastern centre of furniture making in London in the eighteenth century was in the area from St. Paul's Churchyard in the City to Aldersgate Street. The work undertaken in those shops varied from the very high class to respectable middle-of-the-road pieces for bourgeois homes but, in general, it had more in common with the high quality trade of the West End of London than with the cheaper East End trade which was to develop in the nineteenth century. According to the 1801 census there were still about 60 firms working there. By contrast there was only one noted for Curtain Road (Messrs. Brown, cabinet makers and upholsterers), a street which 50 years later was the nerve centre of the East End trade. The development of a furniture making centre in the East End of London did not come from an eastward shift of the respectable firms in the St. Pauls / Aldersgate St. area but rather from the development of new small workshops making cheaper types of furniture in the Bethnal Green, Shoreditch and Hoxton area.

The timber trade

This new development began in the early years of the nineteenth century with the opening of the East India and West India docks. Timber yards and saw mills, which sold and prepared the woods imported through those docks, sprang up nearby and some furniture makers moved near their sources of raw materials. The opening of the Regents Canal in 1820 accelerated this development. Not all timber yards and saw mills were on the banks of the Regents Canal; many were further in, in the main furniture making streets themselves. The yards and mills mainly supplied a small but growing number of 'trade working masters' who worked to orders sub-contracted to them by larger establishments. These firms were small, usually employing between two to five men or boys. There were some firms in the East End which sold direct to retailers but they were in the minority.

Garret masters

The East End trade was distinguished by large numbers of furniture makers who worked on their own. It was relatively easy to set up in business in a small way. Little capital outlay was necessary on tools and furniture makers needed only to buy sufficient timber to make up one piece at a time. The wood was cut to size in a mill and made up in a small workshop or at home as quickly and cheaply as possible. The furniture was then sold in order to buy more wood to make a further item and so on. The move from worker to independent master was so easy to make that many skilled craft workers only considered it when they hit hard times and could not obtain employment in quality shops which paid good wages. Many found themselves in just such a situation in the harsh economic times of the 1830s and 1840s and the small master system rapidly took root. It was not a greatly profitable way of working but this mattered little to those scores of petty producers who, either on their own or with a few unskilled assistants (usually boys), hoped to eke out an existence.

These small masters frequently worked in their own homes, all too often only a room or garret, hence the term 'garret master' by which they were known. They sometimes made to orders given by the 'warehousemen'; sometimes they worked without orders, speculatively 'hawking' their goods on a barrow from one warehouse to another until they were sold. The later it was on a Saturday, the more desperate they became. It was common for goods to be sold at a loss, so desperate were the garret masters to pay their assistants, buy new materials to keep them in business, as well as to buy food for their families in the coming week. Many garret masters employed strong young boys to help them but others could not even afford their cheap labour. Instead they used the free labour of their own children. Whereas the skilled West End furniture makers in the 'respectable' trade deferred marriage and children, the East End garret master planned to have several children and as soon as possible. It was not unusual to have six children, all of whom were set to work as soon as they were old enough — and that might only be six years of age.

The small independent master and very small firms represented the bulk of East End trade throughout the nineteenth century. The 1851 census shows that the average East End workshop employed between one and seven workers, as well as indicating a wide range of specialisations. In Curtain Road alone there were 66 furniture makers, including cabinet makers, carvers, cabinet carvers, and upholsterers, looking glass frame makers, chair makers and french polishers as well as a cabinet maker's porter, an upholsterers's clerk, a picture dealer and a brass manufacturer who probably supplied metal fixtures and fittings for the trade.

The ages of these furniture makers in Curtain Road ranged from 10 to 77; the youngest, George Gibbs, worked as a 'passer up' to a carver while the old man, William Bradbear was a cabinet maker who ran his own firm. His two sons probably worked for him as journeymen, together with John Smith and an apprentice, Henry Allen, who lived in the same house. Some of the furniture makers had been born in the East End while others came from different parts of the capital. Some hailed from further afield. Approximately 25 per cent were born outside London; they came from Yorkshire, Devon, Essex, Northampton, Shropshire, Norfolk, Dorset, Bristol, Liverpool, Worcester and the Isle of Wight. A 34 year old Polish upholsteress, Sophie Jacobs, was also recorded in Curtain Road but it was noted that she was only a 'visitor'.

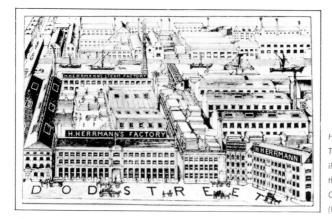

H. Hermann's Steam Factory, Dod Street, E14 1891

*Taken from their advertisement in **The Cabinet Maker** October 1891, this illustration shows how large manufactories were situated on local waterways so that timber could be delivered by boat. Hermann's factory was on Limehouse Cut which linked docks at Limehouse Basin to the River Lea.*
(Photo Studios)

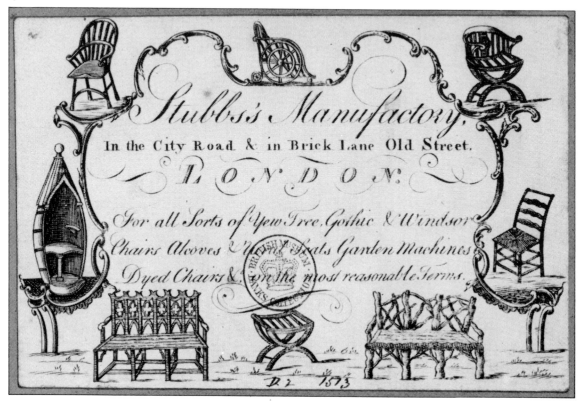

Tradecard for John Stubb's Manufactory, City Road and Brick Lane, E1 1798-9
(Banks Collection, British Museum)

Saw mill: James Latham Ltd. c.1955
(James Latham plc)

James Latham Ltd., 120, Curtain Road, EC2 c.1920
James Latham has been one of East London's largest and most reputable timber merchants for over 150 years. In the 1920s they moved from their premises in Curtain Road to Lea Bridge Wharf, Clapton where they still are today.
(James Latham plc)

Sawing timber: James Latham Ltd. c.1970
Until quite recently hardwoods were imported into London as logs and then cut into planks and kiln or air dried. Today almost all hardwoods are cut into planks in the country of origin.
(James Latham plc)

King John's Court, EC2 1919
Many photographs of the area show evidence of furniture making in the street.
(Greater London Photographs Library)

2-12, Ducal Place, E2 1954
Signs such as this one can still be seen in the area today.
(Greater London Photographs Library)

The Rise and Rise of Curtain Road 1870-1918

By 1861 about 30 per cent of all London furniture makers worked in the East End with the Curtain Road, Old Street area of Shoreditch the main centre of the trade. By the 1870s East London had superseded the West End as the largest furniture making area, both in terms of workers employed and number of establishments. So well established was the trade by that decade that the *Furniture Gazette* noted R. Laddell & Son of Hackney Road specialising as debt collectors to the furniture trade. Firms gradually moved further east within Shoreditch itself and into Bethnal Green as well as north of Old Street into Hoxton. P. G. Hall has pointed out that the french polishers were the only craft group not to spread out from the immediate vicinity of Curtain Road. By 1901 the main furniture making area was along Bethnal Green Road and Hackney Road as well as Curtain Road. It had also spread north of the Regent's Canal, towards Hackney.

The East End trade grew as the sub-contracting system expanded between 1870 and 1890. The large West End firms caved in with the competition of cheap goods from the East End and were no longer able to make all the goods they retailed. Their decline was rapid: by the late 1880s, for instance, Maple & Co. made less than 10 per cent of the goods they sold under their own label.

The variety of work produced in the East End remained as great as ever. The Booth survey of 1887 noted:

> From the East End workshops ... produce goes out of every description, from the richly inlaid cabinet that may be sold for £100, or the carved chair that can be made to pass as rare 'antique' workmanship, down to the gipsy table that the maker sells for 9s a dozen, or the cheap bedroom suites and duchesse tables that are now flooding the market.

There is some evidence of the hours worked at this time. The variety was almost as great as the type of work produced or the structures of the firms. That variety came mainly from the amount of work available. The wages book of a Mr Henzleit or Hensleit (he spelled his name two different ways) shows that in 1884 he worked weekly hours varying between 35 to 70 hours and in 1891 between 44 and 67½ hours.

Jewish workers

The cheap bedroom suites and *duchesse* tables referred to in the Booth survey were the speciality of Jewish firms which had greatly increased in number with the massive Jewish immigration into East London in 1881-6.

The Jewish community in London dates back to the seventeenth century. Political upheavals of the eighteenth and nineteenth centuries brought new immigrants who settled in the already established Jewish community in the east of the City, concentrating in particular areas; by 1881 nearly 20 per cent of the population of certain parts of Whitechapel was Jewish. To this was added the large numbers of immigrants, fleeing persecution, particularly in Poland and Russia, in the years 1881-6. About 20-30,000 European Jews came to London in those years and many settled in Whitechapel, near the docks where they landed. The area offered a common culture, including language and religion, in an alien new world. Some of the immigrants had woodworking skills learned in their villages at home but many were completely green and unskilled. Those highly skilled furniture makers found jobs readily enough or borrowed a little capital and set up on their own, relying on the quality of their work to sell it. Others less talented or with little or no training were prepared to accept almost starvation wages in return for a job where they could pick up a few basic skills.

Unable to speak English, Jewish immigrants were extremely vulnerable to exploitation. However, the Jewish community had strong traditions of philanthropy and looking after its own. The Jewish Board of Guardians (a charitable organisation set up in 1859 to help the poor in the Jewish community) encouraged the new immigrants to join existing firms, rather than set up independently. Nevertheless, it was as easy to set up as an independent master in the 1880s and 1890s as it had been in the 1840s. A reporter for the Booth survey noted that '...a pounds worth of tools and a second pound in cash starts many cabinetmakers on the career of independent worker, and double that amount will often convert him into an employer'. It

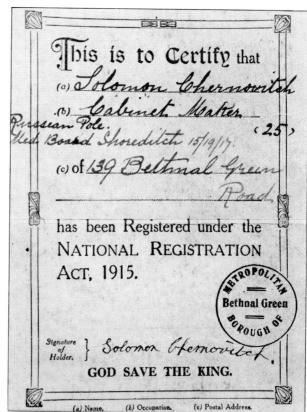

Registration documents relating to Solomon Chernovitch
(Documentary Photography Archive, Manchester)

M. Doctors & Co., 8 Bacon Street, E2 c.1920
(Documentary Photography Archive, Manchester)

was a better alternative than starvation and it was one taken up by many of the Jewish immigrants.

The Jewish Board of Guardians discouraged youths from entering tailoring, boot making and cigarette making in an attempt to keep down the percentage of Jews in those trades because there was considerable hostility to the new immigrants whom, it was claimed, were taking jobs away from Gentiles. In about 1890, for every Jew working in the furniture trade there were 25 working in tailoring. By 1930, however, the ratio was one to nine. In the 1880s and 1890s furniture making came fourth in the list of occupations of the Jewish working class. By 1901 it was second.

Parents were encouraged to get their children some sort of training. The Board found places for youths in furniture workshops and tried to ensure that they were well treated. Oral testimony from both Sam Clarke and Alfred Alexander tell of the representatives of the Board visiting the workshops and overseeing their placements. In Alexander's case his mother was already receiving help from the Board because she was a widow. The Board's recognition of the necessity of a craft training was in advance of that of the trade as a whole. Apprenticeship, in the traditional sense of the word, namely a seven year full craft training in exchange for a sum of money, known as a premium, from the parents or guardian, had virtually disappeared in the West End, let alone the East End. Indeed, the fact that no such apprenticeships were necessary was part of the East End way of working : boys only needed partial skills to get by in most workshops. Nevertheless, the Jewish Board of Guardians constantly emphasised that if boys were to get on in life, the more training the better. If they were ever to move out of the cheaper end of the trade into better quality work then they needed all the skills they could muster. The Board insisted on a five year training, paid a premium to the master and also loaned money for the purchase of tools. Many of these 'apprentices' were paid wages — albeit extremely low wages — whilst they were learning their trade. Most boys entered firms straight from school in the normal way, having been taught some woodworking skills at the Jewish Free School or the local Board schools.

Most Jewish workers worked in Jewish shops for small employers but the Booth survey found no evidence to suggest that there was a disproportionately large number of small firms in the Jewish section of the trade. One firm which absorbed a huge number of unskilled Jewish workers was Lebus of Tabernacle Street, which was owned by Harris Lebus, himself a Jew. In the late nineteenth century it was estimated that 90 per cent of the Lebus workforce were 'green-

ers', employed at very low wages.

Rather than compete directly with Gentile firms, many Jewish employers chose to specialise. One small specialisation was in bamboo and cane work, production of which switched from West End to East End in about 1890. The Booth survey noted that Germans and Jews from Poland and Lithuania were the main workers in this section of the trade. The vast majority of Jewish furniture makers worked at cabinet making but within that area specialised in *duchesse* tables, pedestal tables and bedroom suites. Jewish firms operated at all levels of the trade. Although associated with the very cheapest end of the market in the nineteenth century, many moved towards better quality production which the Royal Commission on Alien Immigration of 1903 described as the sort 'that the ordinary better paid artisan would use and the ordinary tradesman would buy...'.

Whilst Lebus tended to produce for the cheapest end of the market, firms such as Hille catered for the top end. Founded by Salaman Hille in about 1906, it was one of the few Jewish firms run by a non-craftsman. A university educated man, the refugee Salaman found work in England with a wine company in the City before setting up a firm in Derbyshire Street, Bethnal Green. His passion for furniture was 'all in the brain' according to his daughter Ray, because 'he couldn't handle a hammer'. Nevertheless he managed to mastermind the production of some very high quality pieces and by 1914 his firm, by then in Old Street, employed 80 people, mainly cabinet makers and carvers. He maintained a craft apprenticeship training in his workshop where boys were taught a wide range of skills and worked with quality materials. Unlike many East London employers, Hille insisted that his workers should belong to a trade union. He ran one of the few closed shops in the area: no union card, no job. Hille's customers were mainly Jewish but the price of the furniture meant that it was bought by those living outside the East End in the wealthy suburbs of North London. Other Jewish customers also patronised Jewish makers and retailers, of which there was a considerable array with shops in Whitechapel Road. There customers could chose from firms such as Lobovitch, Hyman, Galinsky, and Dolnisky. Otherwise they could try Caplins or Percy Young on the Commercial Road or Wickhams, the 'Harrods of East London' which was situated in Mile End Road. Other smaller Jewish firms did not sell direct and simply supplied the large Tottenham Court Road stores in the same way as did the small Gentile firms.

The working hours, the use of Yiddish in the workshop, the tradition of making by hand at the bench and the

Port of London Cabinet works, 9-21, Cutler Street, E1
Large manufacturing wholesalers built premises that combined workshops,
office and showrooms.
(Photo Studios)

Lebus's: worker pre 1914
The factory was highly mechanised. People worked on production lines rather
than in workshops.
(Vestry House Museum)

Lebus's factory, Ferry Lane, Tottenham Hale, N17
Lebus's were the first large firm to move out to the Lea Valley where land
was cheap, there was space to expand and the river provided transport for
timber.
(Vestry House Museum)

Snap shots such as these, taken by a group of friends at work, are unusual.
Formal photographs for official purposes are not so telling.

less flattering reputation for the love of gambling, are what is said to have made a Jewish workman. Gentiles were supposed to squander their money and time drinking whereas Jewish workers wasted theirs on gambling. The Jewish working week distinguished some workshops but not all. In the Booth report they are recorded as working Monday to Friday from 7 or 8 a.m. to 7 or 8 p.m. with early closing on Friday to prepare for the Sabbath. There was no work on Saturday and none on Sunday, at least from 8 till dusk. The report notes that this added up to an equivalent amount of working hours to a Gentile workshop and concluded that reports concerning Jews being prepared to work longer hours than Gentiles were mostly due to the 'exaggerations of prejudice'.

Not all Jewish people kept such strict hours; it depended on how orthodox they were as to whether they worked on a Saturday. From oral testimony we know that many could not afford, or did not want, to close on a Saturday. What was more common, especially in the years up to 1914 was that most furniture makers stopped early on a Friday and returned home for the family meal. Some of the men would go straight from the workshop to the Vapour baths in Brick Lane for a ritual bathing before the Sabbath.

From small maker to big business

At the end of the 19th century, the typical East End producer, Jew or Gentile, who supplied the large retail firms through a middleman remained a person with little capital and no machinery who either worked on his own or employed from 3 to 6 people. Timber was still bought from the earnings of the week before or on credit. So hand-to-mouth was their existence that transfer from worker to employer, and vice versa, was rapid, fluid and frequent. Indeed, there was often little difference in the living standards and life styles of the East End small employer and the East End furniture worker.

Besides these very small workshops were some employing 10-15 people as well as several larger firms of between 15-25 people. The latter concentrated on better quality production but the the Booth survey noted that only 5 or 6 of them bought in original designs; the others simply copied the current fashions from rival firms:

It takes time to be original, and to do really new work, and there is no time to spare in the furniture trade in East London.

Making up only a small percentage of the trade in the late 1880s came a few large manufactories, the development of which marked a change in the organisation of the East End trade which would have even greater impact in later years. Three or four large establishments employed between 50 and 190 people each. These sold direct to retailers, in London, in the provinces and in the colonies. These brought together the main furniture crafts under one roof, just as had been the case in the prestigious West End shops, but with one major difference. That difference was that the division of labour prevalent in the East End was continued in these factories which housed large numbers of workers, materials were bought in bulk, production was organised along rational lines and subdivided into small repetitive tasks requiring few skills. In general, there was little incentive for East End employers to expend large sums of capital on machinery when there were local saw mills and cheap labour which kept production costs relatively low. The small number of larger firms noted in the Booth survey, however, were distinguished by the fact that they utilised sawing, planing, moulding, boring, dovetailing and other machines on their own premises. They aimed at large scale and speedy production. In 1897 *The Cabinet Maker and Art Furnisher* described the new premises of Clozenberg & Co., a wholesaler turned manufacturer:

...Messrs. Clozenberg, knowing that half measures are of small avail in these times, decided to lay down a plant which should bear upon every process of manufacture and enable them to produce cleanly-worked and well-finished goods with the greatest rapidity, and, while being superior in every way, at a lower price than heretofore.

In the basement at 80, Gt. Eastern Street now the scene is truly a busy one. Every available inch of space is occupied by timber and modern labour-saving contrivances for its conversion. Sawing, planing, moulding, boring, dovetailing, and other machines are whizzing away, turning out parts of suites by the score with perfect accuracy and finish, while, above, the fitting-up and polishing shops are kept fully employed in completing goods for despatch ... As an illustration of the speed with which they are now able to turn out goods, Mr. Clozenberg informs us that, only recently, they made and delivered — for a single order — fifty bedroom suites in under a fortnight in addition to their ordinary business.

B. Cohen & Sons Ltd., 1 - 19 Curtain Road was another wholesaler to turn to manufacturing. In 1890 *The Cabinet Maker* commented:

It would certainly be difficult to find a more eclectic assortment of all that pertains to house furnishing than is found in Messrs. Cohen's establishment. The goods

Shoreditch Technical Institute: upholstery class 1913
(Greater London Photographs Library)

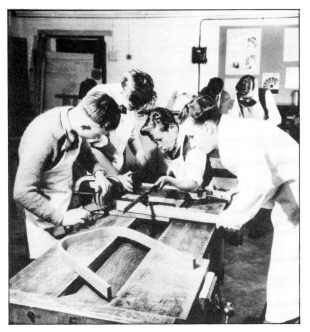

London College of Furniture 1965
(Greater London Photographs Library)

Cabinet making class, Jews Free School 1908
(Greater London Photographs Library)

range from the cheapest — consistent with soundness — extant to the most recherché productions which are to be found in the metropolis, not even excepting aristocratic Bond Street'.

Other large firms included H. Herrmann Ltd. of City Road and Limehouse — 'the largest manufacturers of bedroom suites in Europe'. The biggest of them all was Lebus of Tabernacle Street which by the end of the nineteenth century was the largest furniture making concern in Great Britain. By the time it moved to new premises at Tottenham Hale in 1903 it employed 1000 furniture makers and 45 office staff. This firm moved out in order to expand and mechanise production. Others followed but it was not until the inter-war years that there was a major exodus from the old East End by some of the larger firms anxious to take advantage of cheap land in the Lea Valley.

Importers

Although East London's products continued to reach all corners of the globe, some firms imported furniture. In the 1870s, for instance, Thomas Lane of City Road and Tabernacle Walk imported French cabinets and other foreign furniture as well as acting as agents for 'Patent American Carvings' (presumably machine carvings) and Gense's Universal Spring Mattresses. Imported Indian carved blackwood furniture was sold to Proctor & Co. at 131, Curtain Road, from which address another firm, Perkins & Co., sold a range of black and gold furniture.

Training

The London College of Furniture is well known throughout the country as a centre for training those working in the furniture trade. Its origins go back to about 1899 when the London County Council decided to provide further education for furniture workers. The old Haberdashers' Aske's School in Pitfield Street was acquired and re-named the Shoreditch Technical Institute. Located right in the centre of the furniture making area, it was the first furniture trade school for 'full-time' students working from 8 am to 1 pm. 21 students were admitted when it opened and it grew rapidly thereafter, offering courses which lasted for three years. Such courses were, of course, expensive for employers who could otherwise have been obtaining the products of the boys' labour. This explains why 'full-time' students were relatively few. Once again, it was Jewish employers, mainly the larger ones that could afford it,

who took training most seriously. 'Some adopted a policy of regularly placing one or two of their apprentices on this scheme.

Students were taught drawing, carving, veneering and some theory of construction. Shortly after the Institute opened design was also included as more and more manufacturers realised the importance of this element in a market demanding ever changing styles and types of furniture. Evening classes also catered for those who worked in the trade but other East Enders attended classes there for pleasure and recreation rather than vocational training. In the 1920s and 1930s day release classes were introduced which took place one, two, or three days a week, partly in the trainees' own time and partly in the employers' time. They were mainly intended for apprentices aged 15 to 18. Liaison with the industry consisted of advisory committees including representatives of the employers and employees — as well as the London County Council.

The College also developed as a teacher training establishment; it was seen as essential for future workers to get a good training in craft and woodwork skills while still at school. Its reputation in this sphere was considerable. Shortly before the end of World War II, the teacher training section moved out of East London to Egham in Surrey but the trade training remained where it belonged — in the centre of the furniture making area. In the post war years design was given an added emphasis. In the 1960s the College established an Interior Design department and also developed into the leading educational establishment for musical instrument making in the country. In 1971 it moved to Commercial Road where its programme of over 70 courses range from three year courses in furniture and musical instrument making to short ones in saw doctoring and tool maintenance.

World War I: 1914-1918

The high rate of volunteers for the armed forces amongst furniture makers ushered in many changes in the furniture trade in the years 1914-18. Women were brought in as emergency workers and 'except for the unusually heavy work' undertook every process in the trade as and when it was required of them. Those men who did not join up worked in the trade with women but, once the war was over, the jobs done by women were taken over by the ex-servicemen. In the 1920s the figure for female trade union membership in the furniture trades was only 4 per cent. Women had traditionally worked at upholstery and continued to do so.

They had also been entering french polishing since the late nineteenth century. By 1918 most of the main furniture making trade unions took women polishers as members but within one society at least hostility to female polishers remained strong.

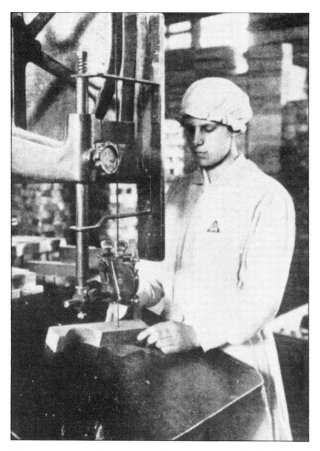
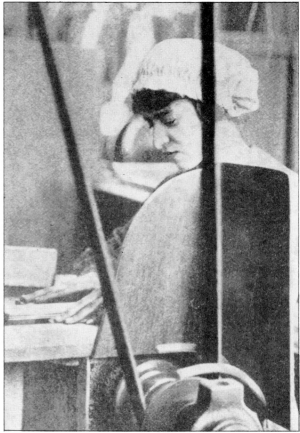

Women operating circular cutter with safety guard: grooving handle cleats. (Photo Studios)

These photographs were reproduced in **The Cabinet Maker**, 17 November 1917. An article on women in the trade concluded: 'We shall need after the war a greatly increased and speeded-up system of production. The scrapping of the large and skilled army of women is almost unthinkable. The introduction of women, like the introduction of machinery, may cause temporary trouble and lead to a revision of popular industrial ideas, but what the war has utilised as emergency labour the interests of national trade will require as a permanent addition to our labour resources.'

The Heyday of the Industry 1918-1939

Consumer demand

The middle and working class market for furniture expanded considerably in the years 1918-1935. Specialist journals and exhibitions concerned with the home multiplied in those years and women's magazines also took a particular interest in the furnishing of the home. The main expansion, however, accompanied the enormous boom in house building after World War I. Those not sufficiently well off to buy a house on a mortgage were also influenced by the images of the 'ideal home' complete with new furniture promoted so vigorously by builders and furniture retailers alike.

A great deal of the increased demand was met by the traditional small workshops which still honeycombed the East End and some furniture was still hawked off barrows at the end of the week — albeit a great deal less than in earlier years. Other firms expanded their premises and increased their output. One of the success stories was Dependable Upholstery of Old Ford, near Victoria Park and the Regents Canal, where it had its own private quay in the 1920s. Founded by Samuel and Jack Breckman in 1907 with a capital of £100, it had capital amounting to £185,000 when it became a public company in 1929. Its Empire Works covered seven acres and included timber yards, a saw mill, a drawing office and an upholstery shop. 400-500 workers produced enough to keep a fleet of 20 lorries busy delivering furniture all over the country.

Although small firms continued to be the mainstay of the East End trade, an increasing number of small makers by-passed the wholesaler and sold direct to retailers and provincial furniture dealers. Improved communications, particularly the use of the telephone, assisted this development. The move towards larger firms which made all their own pieces or organised the production of a complete range of furniture from their own premises also continued to develop. Once again, these also sold direct to retailers, including the large hire purchase establishments such as Cavendish Woodhouse, Times and Great Universal Stores. By 1930 some of the national firms offered credit of three to four years and required no deposit,

thus enabling all but the very poorest of people to purchase furniture they would have believed beyond their reach only a decade or so earlier.

Technology and new materials

Some of the large employers expanded production by introducing machinery. Improvements in wood working machinery, the introduction in 1920 of plywood which was cheap and easy to cut to shape and the rapid spread of electrification in the ensuing decade all facilitated the changeover to machine mass production. Few East End businesses had sites large enough for such expansion, however, and most of the new developments took place in firms which moved out, or had already moved out, to the Lea Valley. These included Lebus, Bluestone and Elvin (from Shoreditch to Walthamstow in 1928), B and I Nathan (from Curtain Road to Hackney in 1928 and on to Walthamstow in 1930) and Beautility (from Bethnal Green to Edmonton in about 1933). By far the largest transfer of furniture firms from the inner East End took place in the years after the completion of the national electricity grid (1927-1934) : at least a dozen firms moved out to the Lea Valley in the years 1935-8.

Once out in the eastern suburbs, these firms introduced machinery for planing, mortising, jointing, dovetailing, moulding, turning, and carving. All the main parts of sideboards, bedsteads, cabinets and chests-of-drawers were produced by wood machinists ready for the cabinet makers to assemble. Indeed, the former workers became as important as the latter: by 1930 the full London rate for wood working machinists was the same as that for cabinet makers, namely 82s 3d for a 47 hour week at time rates. Those makers in the old East End with neither the capital nor the space to install machinery, continued to take advantage of the several specialist wood machine shops which had sprung up in the area for sawing, cutting and planing. Grisley's Mill on Kingsland Road was typical: 'someone came round the local shops every day with a barrow ... They would shout up and you would take down wood that was marked out for

Glebe Veneered Plywood Manufacturing Co., 293-295, Kingsland Road, E8
Advertisement in **The Cabinet Maker**, August 1927
(Photo Studios)

Lebus's, Ferry Lane, N17: polishing lines
Factory processes such as spray polishing still required some degree of
hand-finishing.
(Vestry House Museum)

cuttings and mouldings.' Machine work was somewhat dangerous, with few employers providing effective safety guards: there is an old saying in the trade that you were never a proper machinist until you had at least two fingers chopped off! It was not only machining which was dangerous, other accidents happened in small shops with hot fires and boiling glue pots. Chisels slipped as did hammers. Indeed, the Mildmay Hospital in Austin Street was known as the cabinet makers' hospital because that was where most furniture makers went with their injuries. This, incidentally, was a Church of England Mission hospital and old furniture makers recall having to attend a church service before getting their wounds redressed.

Another threat to the cheap end of the East London trade, based as it was on wood and hand labour, came from 'Lloyd Loom' furniture which was made from twisted paper reinforced with wire and woven on mechanised looms. This remarkable invention was an American one of 1919 but the British franchise was taken up by Lusty & Co. in 1922. Ironically, the Lusty works were in the East End, in Bow, and the firm became a large local employer as the product range became widely known and most homes in Britain owned at least a bedroom chair or a linen basket in this new material.

Unemployment

In the uncertain economic times of the inter-war years unemployment rates in furniture making were never as high as in other East End trades. The increased demand for furniture, especially from the relatively prosperous south-east of the country, gave the trade a filip and offset many of the problems faced by other workers. Until 1930 the furniture trade was one of the most buoyant in the country. But, this does not mean that there was no genuine hardship amongst East End furniture makers . The trade remained notorious for its seasonal unemployment and women, who were for the most part employed in the small upholstery sector, were particularly vulnerable to its seasonal demands. Wider trade depressions also had their impact and the doubt and uncertainty of the 1930s stopped many people buying furniture. Competition was fierce as small and large manufacturers alike fought for survival; both kept down wages in an effort to get goods to the customer more cheaply than the nearest competitor.

Trade took a turn for the worse in the 1930s but there was still a brisk trade in lower priced goods. The larger

employers increasingly turned to manufacturing cheap furniture using machine mass production, with the result that many skilled workers lost their jobs. The first mention of the link between mass production and the unemployment of its skilled members came in the NAFTA journal of 1934 when over 20 per cent of its members were out of work. The union re-doubled its efforts to unionise this sector of the industry, realising at last that they could not afford to ignore the unskilled workers.

Interwood Ltd., 326 Old Street, EC1. 'Modern Veneering Plant'
Advertisement in **The Cabinet Maker**, August 1927
(Photo Studios)

Ray Hille in workshop with carver
In 1940 Hille's Old Street works was destroyed during bombing. Their insurers, Royal Exchange, asked Ray to take on assessing bomb damaged high quality furniture. Around the same time she was recommended by the Victoria & Albert Museum to the City guildhalls to replace bomb damaged furniture. With timber from old wardrobes bought in sale rooms and improvised tools, Ray kept the business going with 'reconstruction work'. (Hille International Ltd.)

Buying secondhand furniture from West End Store
This photograph is one of a series of official pictures documenting the experience of a 'war bride'.
(Imperial War Museum)

World War II: 1939-1945

Many furniture makers fought in World War II. Those who did not were either allocated to war work (mainly done by the larger firms), the production of Utility furniture (mainly done by 'middling' sized firms) or 'reconstruction' work (done by the very smallest firms). Stocks of timber were so great when war broke out in 1939 that there was no apparent shortage of furniture for some time. Two days after the declaration of war, the Ministry of Supply imposed timber control regulations under the Defence of the Realm Acts. By July 1940 all timber supplies to the furniture industry ceased. Production continued to some extent from stocks of timber already held by manufacturers. As shortages increased, so did profiteering. Price controls were brought in by the Government in an attempt to regularize matters. Purchase taxes of a sixth to a third were introduced on many goods, including furniture, to reduce demand as well as raise revenue. Demand however rose as half a million or so marriages continued to take place each year. The price of second hand furniture went through the roof.

Utility furniture

The Government had, in part, been prepared for this crisis and in 1941 introduced 'Standard Emergency Furniture' with standard specifications for all new production being issued to firms already working on government contracts. Within eighteen months the Utility Furniture Scheme was introduced which emphasised good design and the economical use of timber. Utility furniture was only available to newly-weds or people who had been bombed out of their houses and lost all their belongings. Prospective buyers had to get an application form from their local Fuel Office for a permit. Each permit carried 60 units and was valid for three months. The unit value of furniture varied from eight for a wardrobe to one for a kitchen or dining chair. Retailers could only get furniture from a manufacturer against units given over by customers who had made their choice from a catalogue and not from examples held at the shop. Public meetings were held at which designers of Utility furniture made serious attempts to find out what people needed and how furniture was used.

At the end of the war the range of Utility furniture was extended and plans were made to make items available to people outside priority classes. But supply lagged a long way behind demand and price controls continued until 1948.

'Reconstruction'

For the small family firm making furniture, the war brought hardship for those who were judged unsuitable by the Government for war production or the making of 'Utility' goods. Some were lucky to be appointed as 'repairers', undertaking what was called 'reconstruction' work which involved using old furniture and wood to make 'new' pieces. Ray Hille, who by this date had taken over from her father, Salaman, found work assessing bomb-damaged furniture after the firm's Old Street premises were completely destroyed in December 1940. New workshops were obtained in nearby Rivington Street where several of the older employees rejoined her as the firm began the repair of bomb-damaged furniture (mainly Hille pieces) using wood from old bomb-damaged furniture bought at auction. Other firms simply closed as family members joined the forces or else they went into necessary war work.

War work

Many furniture factories were turned over to aircraft production for the duration of the war. Work varied from firm to firm but it included the building of aircraft such as de Havilands, Mosquitoes, Hotspurs and Hansers. Indeed, the Mosquito was known as 'the cabinet makers' plane' because the whole of the fuselage was made of wood. Other work included smaller items such as munitions boxes, tent pegs and bunks for air raid shelters. Work specifically related to the war effort was done by the larger firms to government contracts. The very production of aircraft components

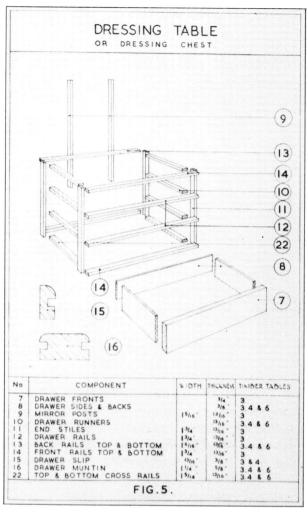

Lebus, Finsbury Works, N17

Advertisement for Utility furniture, **The Cabinet Maker** 19 July 1947

(Photo Studios)

Board of Trade, General Specification for Utility Furniture 1948

Design for Dressing Table

(Photo Studios)

Harris Lebus, Finsbury Works, N17: extension of warehouses to accomodate

aircraft production 1939-45

(Vestry House Museum)

and the active part played in the development of new materials and techniques by the large factories consolidated their position in the trade.

All the war time production in East London was carried out in circumstances which were, to say the least, far from favourable. Many furniture makers were bombed out of their homes as well as their workshops yet, somehow, they managed to obtain makeshift premises, to beg or borrow tools and materials and carry on despite the odds.

Joint Industrial Council (JIC)

The war brought together labour and employers. A Joint Industrial Council (JIC) was established in 1939 and a year later a Furniture Trade Board. Both these organisations brought together under government sponsorship, management and unions to work out policy and decide on wages and conditions. The government also insisted, after some pressure from the unions, that all firms involved in war production, irrespective of size, should be unionised. In 1946, after five years of co-operation the first National Agreement on wages and conditions was signed between the employers and the unions. It established a working week of 44 hours with standard overtime rates, holidays with pay, minimum wage rates for all classes of workers and standard conditions for the training of apprentices and learners including day release.

Women

As in World War I, women took up jobs, including machine sawing previously done by male furniture makers. By 1944 one in four workers in the furniture industry was female. Many women who worked as french polishers before the war transferred to aircraft production. They performed jobs such as picking up and putting in tiny screws which were considered suitable for 'nimble female hands' yet classified as unskilled in terms of pay. Some women worked at assembling aircraft on an equal basis as men — equal that is in everything but payment. The influx of women necessitated a change in the way in which both the furniture trade and women were perceived. Furniture factories were fairly physically demanding places in which to work and in war-time women proved that they were up to the tasks before them. This was not only widely acknowledged but also praised.

After the war, however, there was great pressure on women to return to the home, and certainly to vacate male jobs. Yet, even at the height of women's retrenchment into the home in the 1950s and 60s, women's membership of the furniture trade unions remained as high as 15 per cent (as opposed to only 4 per cent in the 1920s). What those women who remained in the industry lost, however, was the right to work at 'male' jobs in machining and assembly work. After the war women went back to work at their traditional jobs in upholstery and polishing. A few women were allowed to stay on in veneering but, once again, this was because it was considered that female fingers were more nimble than male ones and therefore better suited to the cutting, jointing and matching of veneers.

Warerite Plastics
Advertisement in **The Cabinet Maker**, 4 October 1957
(Photo Studios)

L. Lazarus & Sons Ltd., 'Majority Works', Angel Factory Colony, Edmonton, N18
Advertisement for 'Uniflex' unit bedroom furniture, **The Cabinet Maker**,
11 October 1957
(Photo Studios)

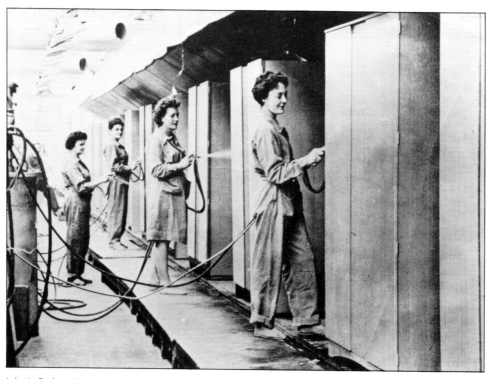

Lebus's, Finsbury Works, N17: Women on polishing line 1950s
(Sissy Lewis)

Picking up the Pieces: 1945-1975

The general post-war picture is one of the decline of the traditional East End trade as cheap production became increasingly concentrated in the Lea Valley. In the immediate post-war years, however, both large and small producers were faced with difficulties such as restrictions on consumer spending, the rationing of new materials and the lack of any export trade. The market was slack and several firms failed to weather the storm. In order to survive, the larger firms turned increasingly to mechanical mass production while the smaller ones in the traditional East End specialised in order to survive.

The Lea Valley firms

The large factories in the outer suburbs retained and extended the intensive division of labour characteristic of the old East End trade but brought together all aspects of furniture making within a single firm. Entire product ranges were made from start to finish, using new materials, such as plywood, and new technology, such as panel construction and electrically driven machinery. These firms continued to flourish in the 1950s and 1960s when improved techniques and the use of particleboard introduced further de-skilling of jobs while increasing productivity. By 1959 the number of firms working in the East and North East of London had fallen by half and the labour force by over a third compared with pre-war levels. Most of the big firms concentrated on high volume production of modularised chipboard cabinets. However, excess capacity and price wars were a feature of the 1970s when bad management was endemic and little or no attention was paid to product development, including design. The trade was to pay for this dearly. The 1979 depression gave foreign manufacturers, especially those from Germany, the chance they had been waiting for. They soon made decisive inroads into the British market and foreign imports of well designed and efficiently marketed products now stand at over 30 per cent of sales. Competition was cut throat and many firms did not survive. The London trade has been decimated, almost obliterated, in the last decade. Many of

the big names of British furniture and of the East End, such as Lebus and Beautility, are now out of business. Others seem doomed to follow unless radical changes in government and management policies take place.

The old East End

The old East End could not compete with the products of the large factories. Extensive war damage meant that many firms did not start up again; some felt they could not make the transition from war work to furniture making proper under such intense competition, others set up only to suffer heavy losses and close down. What remained of the furniture trade — and it was quite considerable — became more specialised than before. The firms which best survived were those which produced the better quality work. There had always been firms which made good quality 'period' pieces; they now came to dominate the East End trade. Increasing mechanisation in the Lea Valley trade made the gap even greater between furniture making in 'outer' and 'inner' East London, as the latter increasingly centred on the reproduction trade. The work never pretended to be anything but reproduction pieces yet some antique dealers have recently described how, as younger men, they visited the East End to buy furniture which they later sold in their shops as antiques. This was, and still is, machine assisted rather than mechanised production, if not mainly hand production, which is based on either one-off orders at the top end or batch production lower down.

Competition was hard in the furniture trade which was in the grip of retailers who virtually dictated what would and would not be offered on the domestic market. Many firms looked to the expanding contract market for salvation, involving as it did, large orders of furniture for offices, schools, hospitals, canteens etc. Firms such as Hille, which had moved out of the inner East End after the war to more up-to-date premises in Lea Bridge Road pioneered, and rapidly obtained an international reputation for the development of modern design in this field. Others like Palatial Ltd. of Wick

C.T.H. Furniture Works, 139, Hackney Road, E2 1966 (Greater London Photographs Library)

Gunham Plastics Ltd., and Sage and Stanley, 49-51 Hoxton Square, N1 1971
(Greater London Photographs Library)

Lane, Old Ford (formerly Lubelsky and now Lucas Furniture Systems) produced high quality hand finished furniture.

As the East End trade continued to decline, many firms were forced to re-consider their future as they hit financial difficulties. Some old premises were torn down as parts of Shoreditch, Hoxton and Tower Hamlets were redeveloped in the 1960s while, at the same time, there were further government incentives to industry to relocate to New Towns and other greenfield sites. But the dilemma remained for those firms involved in hand finished reproduction work, namely that they depended on a whole network of skills available in the East End. Furthermore, workers were often quite reluctant to leave their community, even for the promised lands of Harlow or Watford.

Contract furnishing

The post-war welfare state created many new hospitals, universities and other large public buildings; property developers erected high rise offices on bomb damaged sites in the nearby City of London; hotels were put up all over the country with the aid of government grants aimed at boosting the tourist industry. For a number of the larger firms in the old East End, the contract market represented their main means of survival.

The stranglehold of the retailers and the intense competition in the domestic market led Palatial Ltd., 616, Wick Lane, into office furnishing in the late 1940s. Around the same time Evans of London Ltd., 225 Old Ford Road, moved into university and hospital furnishing. In 1957 Morris and Rhoda Serlin left the family business to set up MAS Contracts which specialised initially in furniture for hotels. Another advantage in moving away from the domestic market was that manufacturers were able to develop more innovative product design. As Paul Lucas of Palatial (now Lucas Furniture Systems) has explained:

...we had to be more concerned with product development rather than pleasing a market which hardly knew its own mind and was busily engaged in scrapping with themselves as to exclusivity and mark-up. If you served one group you were told you could not serve another — this really made nonsense of a logical design concept.'

Upholstery workshop, Teesdale Street, E2 1986
(David Dilley)

The Industry Now

The 'repro' trade

Today's trade is largely concentrated in the Hackney Road district, between Hackney and Tower Hamlets. The dominant pattern is still one of scores of small workshops (only seven businesses employ between 30 and 70 people). Many are still family concerns but whilst the names might be the same, the East End trade is not.

The whole furniture sector has been in decline since about 1960, with an extreme downturn since 1979. However, the East End reproduction trade declined at a much faster rate than any other sector. The problems are manifold. Firm after firm has gone bust; many of the 'big' names associated with prouder days in the trade are amongst the victims. In 1961 just over 5,000 people were employed in the industry in Hackney and Tower Hamlets but today it is estimated that the number is only half, and is continuing to fall. Cramped, dusty and dingy workshops are the order of the day. Furthermore, many of the small firms which remain are hostile to trade unionism, preferring to employ staff on a 'self-employed' basis thereby avoiding compliance with employment and health legislation. In consequence conditions in many workshops and small factories are bad and wage levels, particularly for the young, are very low. The trade faces an insecure future. The traditional outlets for reproduction furniture have been the privately owned provincial retail firms in city centre sites. These are now on the decline as they are replaced by multiples and out-of-town super stores selling cheap 'repro' furniture from abroad. Recent surveys have emphasised that the main problem facing furniture manufacturers in the area were: low productivity and profits, inadequate premises, cash shortages and poor marketing resources as well as a lack of capital investment in machinery or new product lines, design initiatives and skilled workers. Skill is in very short supply and is mainly concentrated in the older section of the workforce, many of whom are now approaching retirement. Since apprenticeship and other hands-on training has virtually disappeared because young people do not find furniture making an attractive trade to enter. The next few years will see a significant loss in craft knowledge and skill in the East End trade. One survey commented on the atmosphere of 'cheerful muddle' in firms which compete for orders in a fiercely competitive international market. To survive in such a market huge capital investment is called for as well as clear marketing strategies and networks, whereas export strategies and the promotion of goods have never been taken very seriously in the East End trade.

Faced with low profit margins on the one hand, and competition from Taiwan on the other, life is difficult in the reproduction trade. There have been no major developments in mechanisation and batch production rarely exceeds 50 pieces. This means that the main way to economise in production is on labour. Hand labour is, of course, cheaper in Taiwan than in East London, with disastrous consequences for the London trade. It is ironical indeed that the main threat now comes from a sweated industry with many similarities to that of mid-nineteenth century Curtain Road. The most recent threats to workers' jobs come not from the East but high-tec developments in the West: from the micro chip, namely computer controlled shaping, boring and routing machinery; computer aided size co-ordination and design as well as retailing linked by computer to production.

New initiatives

There are a few glimmers of light in the gloom which hangs over the collapse of what was once one of East London's best known industries. Several new schemes have aimed at rescuing an ailing industry. Financial assistance and research have been provided by the Greater London Enterprise Board but since the abolition of the Greater London Council in 1986 there have been no new projects on the furniture trade from this sector. This work has now been taken on by various agencies in the boroughs concerned. At present Hackney Council's Economic Development Unit is leading the way in this area, Hackney having made the furniture industry a priority for assistance.

Three types of grant are available to firms in the

Rebecca Myram, 37 Cremer Street, E2 1987
Recently qualified in furniture design at the Royal College of Art, Rebecca
Myram creates furniture in ash and oak which 'people can relate to'. She
produces one off pieces using a special steam technique. Her aim is to get into
small batch production.
(Hackney Economic Development Unit)

borough; two year rent grants on new leases, 50 per cent renovation costs to property in industrial improvement areas and 'setting up' grants of £1,000 to all co-operatives. Certain conditions are attached to grants, which are as follows:

1. Firms must pay at least £3 an hour
2. Firms must offer full negotiating rights to the furniture union FTAT
3. Firms must comply with the Race Regulations Act, Sex Equality Act and Health & Safety regulations
4. Firms must give all employees contracts of employment
5. Firms must not employ casual or self-employed workers
6. Firms must not be in direct competition with other Hackney firms

Hackney has been working closely with the furniture union FTAT, Tower Hamlets Council and the London College of Furniture. Several joint schemes have resulted, one of which involves the employment by the two boroughs of a consultant from the College to promote the manufacture of 'designer furniture'.

Designer furniture

In the last few years numerous designer-makers have set up workshops in the East End and the number is rising steadily. There are many problems facing this section of the industry, the greatest of which is finding outlets for their work. The solution for the majority is to work to commission, most of their clients being architects and interior designers. Many, like Rebecca Myram, would like to expand into small batch production. Networks to support these makers are of crucial importance as is proven by the pioneering work of IDF, the Independent Designers Federation, a national organisation that has several members in East London. Andrew Kindler, whose workshop is at Limehouse, articulated the views of other designer-makers when he stated:

A craftsman can work anywhere in England and still reach his customers. I find the East End/ Docklands ideally placed for access to raw materials, tools and suppliers to the trade.

Steval, 18 Ashwin Street, E8 1987
One of Hackney's 60 co-ops, Steval is a three person, family co-op making small batches of good quality reproduction furniture.
(Hackney Economic Development Unit)

Futon Trading, Bayford Street, E8 1987
Many companies such as this one have started to manufacture the cotton futon mattress and pine sofabed base. This company, set up by Dave and Corrine Rechais, now employs four people.
(Hackney Economic Development Unit)

Chapter Two

DISTRIBUTION AND MARKETING

Wholesale trade

Direct trading

Retailers

Export trade

Design

Hire purchase

Exhibitions

Advertising

Window display

Catalogues

Petrol Lorry

Advertisement in **The Furniture Record***, 25 August 1905*

Motorised vehicles like this one came into use at the turn of the century.

(Photo Studios)

DISTRIBUTION AND MARKETING

The process of furniture making cannot be separated from the business of selling furniture. Since the expansion of a merchant class in the sixteenth century, a growing division has occurred between those who make and those who sell. The producers have consequently become almost completely detached from the consumers and therefore increasingly dependent on the middlemen whose contact with and knowledge of the market has enabled them to dominate manufacturing. The role of the middlemen — wholesalers and retailers — has been particularly significant in the development of the East London furniture trade.

The multitudinous small makers who constituted a large part of the industry until the middle of this century were not large enough to handle their own marketing and distribution. In the nineteenth century big wholesale operations grew up in and around Curtain Road that not only sub-contracted work but also created outlets for goods made in the locality. Such firms were suppliers rather than makers of furniture. By the twentieth century larger manufacturers were in a position to supply shops directly and the importance of these 'non-producing' wholesalers declined. Since the end of the last century most retailers have been supplied by 'manufacturing wholesalers'.

Clashes of interest often occurred between wholesalers and retailers. In 1896 an association of retailers and wholesalers in the London area, the Cabinet Trades Federation, was formed, partly with the purpose of dealing with 'occasional difficulties between different sections of the trade'. By 1929 over 80 per cent of its membership was made up of manufacturing wholesalers in East London. The National Federation of the Furniture Trades, another professional body, had separate sections for retailers and wholesalers. The most common source of conflict was the question of who was entitled to sell to the public; retailers have fiercely defended their right to do so and attacked any wholesaler known to sell direct.

Furniture retailing expanded with the growth of the suburbs and the increased purchasing power of the middle classes and then later the working classes. The development of hire purchase trading and other sorts of credit facilities greatly enhanced demand. By the middle of the nineteenth century the Tottenham Court Road area was established as the centre of the retail furniture trade with department stores like Shoolbreds and Oeztmanns and specialist furnishing shops such as Maples and Heals. Lavish decor and dazzling displays attracted clientele from all over the country, as shopping developed as a leisure activity. East End makers supplied these and other quality West End stores including Hamptons, Libertys and Waring and Gillows, both directly and indirectly from wholesale warehouses. During the 1880s Maples is known to have been supplied by a thousand East End firms. By the turn of the century multiple — or chain — shops were growing rapidly in London and the suburbs. During the decades to come firms like Times, Hackney Furnishing Company, Smarts, Bolsoms, Perrings and Catesbys were major distributors of East London furniture. There were also many independent furniture retailers in London and the provinces who bought from the East End, Curtain Road having become the mecca of retail buyers throughout the country.

Various methods of direct selling which cut out the middleman's profit were practised by East End firms. The most common one, making to order for individual clients, was a feature of the East London trade, especially amongst Jewish firms. Some large workshops had showrooms where they sold to the public; others operated mail order services or specialised in contract furnishings.

Methods of marketing became increasingly more sophisticated from the late nineteenth century with the development of the media. Newly established women's magazines, trade journals and local newspapers greatly increased opportunities for advertising. Prior to this time the most effective means of promoting goods and building up custom was to take a stand at an exhibition or trade fair. During the 1870s printed catalogues began to be produced which enabled dealers to illustrate complete ranges of stock. Catalogues designed for the retail trade tended to illustrate rows of 'disembodied' furniture; those intended for user-consumers were more lavish and often included appealing pictures of room sets designed to enhance the furniture. As women's maga-

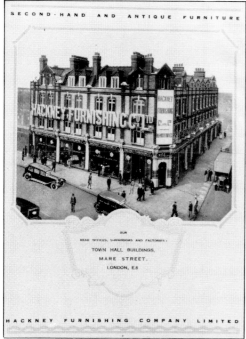

Hackney Furnishing Co. Ltd., Mare Street, E8 1920s
The largest furniture store in East London, with branches in the West End and
the suburbs, the Hackney Furnishing Company overstretched itself in the 1930s
and was taken over by Great Universal Stores.
(Photo Studios)

J. Collier & Sons Ltd., 134-142, Clapham Road, SW9 c.1935
Established in 1852, Colliers had a small chain of furniture stores in south
London.
(Photo Studios)

Bartholomew & Fletcher, 217-218 Tottenham Court Road 1930s
Established in 1843, Bartholomew & Fletcher sold high quality reproduction
work and antique furniture.
(Photo Studios)

J. Liversidge & Son Ltd., 196, Old Street, EC1
*Advertisement in **The Cabinet Maker**, June 1904*
One of the chief suppliers of transport to the furniture trade, road vehicles such
as those made by Liversidge's were used to transport goods around the
metropolis. For longer journeys rail was used.
(Photo Studios)

zines and books on furnishing and decorating the home were popularised towards the end of the century, so some firms adopted the language and format of these publications; by the 1930s hints from Hollywood stars had become features in furniture catalogues. Ideal homes could be created more easily in two rather than three dimensions, but similar techniques were applied to the design of showroom and window displays in shops.

The way in which furniture was sold came to be almost as important as the product itself; furniture design was as much to do with marketing as graphic design. A leading West End retailer once described the East End trade as 'anything to order'; adaptability and sensitivity to the demands of the market were characteristics of the industry in this area. Infinite diversification of styles and types was made possible by the structure of the trade and facilitated by technological advances in the nineteenth century that produced cheap veneers, mouldings and carving for ornamentation.

Every conceivable kind of furniture has been produced in the workshops and factories of East London: from kitchen chairs for Buckingham Palace to overmantels for Whitechapel tenement blocks; from folding furniture for the 1890s export market to 'knockdown' furniture for the 1950s domestic market. It was sold to colonial princes and to suburban clerks; to Australian settlers and to English marchionesses. The following pages will explain how distribution and marketing have been carried out, first of all examining four methods of distribution: wholesale, retail, export and direct selling, and then discussing some of the most important marketing techniques.

Wholesale trade

Curtain Road and the adjacent streets, was the heart of the wholesale trade. Giant warehouses were built in the 1870s as businesses expanded and sites became available following redevelopment of the area by the Metropolitan Board of Works. In December 1877 the firm of H. Vaughan opened new premises at 70, Curtain Road which 'provided every requisite for business purposes'. There was a dry spacious basement for packing. The ground floor was 'entered by wide folding doors with windows on each side, formed of two magnificent sheets of plate glass, each at least eight by ten feet, well adapted for the display of goods...' It also housed the office. On the first floor there were three rooms; the first was another showroom, the second a private reception room occupied by Mr Vaughan himself where 'will be dispensed the

judicious hospitalities which on certain occasions, give a moderate impulse to business transactions', and the third was a store for upholstery materials. There were two rooms on the third floor; the front one housed a polishing shop and the back one an upholstery shop. The whole building had 'speaking tubes fitted all over the place', a very modern invention. As Booth pointed out in 1889:

Many of these warehouses are simply showrooms, some of great size, a few have workshops of different kinds on the upper floors, but for the most part the buildings flanking 'the Road' are places of sale and not of manufacture. The various technical processes are carried out in back streets more or less remote...

The warehousemen prospered from and maintained the economic conditions of the East End trade. Their work was two-fold; they supplied retailers with stock and they organised manufacturing. Dealers saved on having to pay rent for workshop space and avoided the responsibility of managing labour directly. By forcing small makers into competition, the wholesaler could obtain goods at prices lower than the cost of maintaining a large workshop or factory. It is these men who are credited with having extended the market for locally manufactured goods. Magnificent displays of stock, providing a great selection of designs, attracted retail buyers from all parts of Britain and overseas; a range of anything less than, for example, 40 bedroom suites would have seemed disappointing. Large catalogues were distributed, some of which offered space for overprinting with the name of a client's shop, or representatives were sent out with photographs of their wares. The quantity of stocks carried was so great that in some cases Victorian lines were still available in the 1930s.

Profits made by wholesalers varied in accordance with capital investment and entrepreneurial skill. Booth claimed that there was no evidence of dealers, except in a few cases, making excessive profits. A witness to the Select Committee on the Sweating System in 1888 did not share this view. He described how C. & R. Light Ltd. sold a dining table for 34s 6d, 'a common pine table with birch legs, 5ft by 3ft 6in, with one flap to it... what is called a common dining table in the trade'. Such a table would have cost the maker, it was claimed, about 13s for materials (5s 6d for the top, 4s for the legs, 1s 4d for the screw and 2s for fixings) and would have taken two days to make. Half a day could be spent hawking. Although the maker would have asked 18s for the piece he would have been lucky to get more than 16s. Light's would have spent 2s on polishing, the remainder of the 34s 6d was their profit. The witness stated:

Law Brothers, 43-45, Great Eastern Street and 60, Curtain Road, EC2
Advertisement in **The Furniture Record**, 25 August 1905
Law Brothers premises were typical of prosperous wholesalers' warehouses in this area. Their specialities are listed in the advertisement.
(Photo Studios)

C. & R. Light Ltd., Curtain Road, EC2
Advertisement in **The Furniture Record**, 25 August 1905
(Photo Studios)

McCarthy's, 179-181 Bethnal Green Road, E2 1976
*During the 1920s and 30s McCarthy's advertised regularly in the **Hackney Gazette**.*
(Greater London Photographs Library)

J.T. Norman, 57 Great Eastern Street, EC2
Advertisement for their 'Furnishing Guide', **The Cabinet Maker**, March 1886.
It was common for wholesalers to supply catalogues to retail customers overprinted in the client's name.
(Photo Studios)

We want to point out the unfairness of the system which prevails in these dealing firms; they get the whole of the profits; the workman has scarcely anything for his labour. Simply by buying furniture, and transmitting it to the warerooms, the dealer gets a large percentage on the goods, and the man that really produces the article gets nil.

As mechanisation and larger units of production developed, the role of this type of wholesaler diminished in importance. The response of some firms was to expand manufacturing. In 1931 the *New Survey of London Life and Labour* commented on the decline of the non-producing wholesaler. The 1946 *Board of Trade Working Party Report on Furniture* found that the role played by wholesalers was small, but that in certain branches of the trade, notably in the distribution of occasional furniture, a large part of the business still passed through their hands. Since the Second World War these wholesalers have continued to provide a link between the small maker and the small retailer in the suburbs and the provinces.

Direct trading

Besides selling to retail outlets, some wholesale suppliers also sold direct to the public. Manufacturing wholesalers such as W.E. Hardy of 132, Curtain Road, who advertised in local papers like the *Hackney Gazette*, sold direct using an 'Easy Hire System'. Wm. Wallace & Co. of 151-155, Curtain Road, described themselves as 'Wholesale House Furnishers and Decorators'. They undertook complete furnishing schemes as well as supplying furniture. The list of testimonials from satisfied customers printed in their catalogue, including the Dowager Duchess of Marlborough, the Marquis of Tweedale, Viscountess Molesworth etc., suggests that they supplied large houses with bulk orders of everyday furniture, such as their 'Indispensable Corner Wardrobe'. Respectable firms like J.S. Henry, 287-291, Old Street, discreetly sold to the public via their agents in Paris.

In the inter-war years, as professional codes of conduct were laid down, the issue of direct trading was hotly debated. Retailers complained that since the war there had been a great deal of propaganda against the middleman and consequently a growing popularity amongst the public for this method of trading. The difference between wholesale and retail prices was in some cases as much as 40 or 50 per cent. The public demand for goods at wholesale prices stimulated the growth of agencies that operated 'direct shopping systems'. Such firms published

and circulated promotional literature to secure clients. The retail profession was so keen to accuse manufacturers of unfair trading that even supplying furniture direct to golfing partners was criticised.

Buying direct from someone you knew was a common practice amongst many people who lived in or who were brought up in East London. For those who prospered and moved away in the inter-war years, it became prestigious, especially it seems amongst Jewish newly-weds, to order bespoke furniture from East End firms, Hille and Epstein's being the most fashionable. Firms such as Chippendale Workshops fully exploited the demand for bespoke furniture by opening a showroom in the West End where they could take orders and also sell ready made goods direct to the public. Some small firms surviving from this period still make quality furniture to order for bespoke customers today. There are also a number of young makers working on their own who are discovering a growing market for this type of trade. Edward Sanson, for instance, on completion of his training at the London College of Furniture set up a workshop with a local authority grant in 1985. Much of his work is for individual clients who want wall units or video cabinets because they have awkward spaces in their homes for which standardised mass produced units are unsuitable. Although this kind of furniture usually costs the customer a little more than purchasing it from a retailer, an increasing number of people are choosing to buy in this way.

It has always been permissible for wholesalers and manufacturers to directly supply contract customers. The growth of commercial and public organisations in the nineteenth century enabled many large firms to prosper from the contract trade. In the post-war period this market has been the only means of survival for larger firms in the area.

Retailers

Retailers have traditionally justified their profits by claiming that they offer a service to the consumer. As the middle class market grew in the nineteenth century they took on the same kind of advisory role that interior decorators performed for the aristocracy. By the 1920s this had crystallised into what C.A. Richter, then President of the National Association of Retail Furnishers, called the 'art of homemaking'. In an address reported in *The Cabinet Maker* in July 1927 he described the job of the retail furnisher as follows:

...he should be the furnishing artist par excellence. Unless he makes some attempt to be this he does not

J.S. Henry Ltd., 287-291, Old Street, EC1
Advertisement in **The Cabinet Maker**, June 1904
(Photo Studios)

Hille Sideboard made for Mrs Sophia Baron 1931
Mrs Baron had all her furniture made by Hille when she got married. 'My father
and I went along to the Hille factory and had a chat with old Mr Hille, a great
character with a white beard and a very autocratic manner — he knew he was
good and told you so. I told him I wanted walnut for the dining-room and
bedroom suites and a blond wood, preferably birds-eye maple for the
living-room. I also told him I wanted simple, clean lines with no 'fancy
work'...my only other specific request was for chairs with solid unpierced slats.
He showed me some woods and I chose from them, but left the designs to
him!'
(Chris Shelton)

Wm. Wallace & Co., 151-155 Curtain Road, EC2
High-class Inexpensive Drawing Room Furniture: catalogue c.1895
This wholesale firm produced lavish catalogues aimed at the public.
(Silver Studio Collection)

justify his existence. He should do something more than rent a few thousand square feet of showroom space and fill it with a miscellaneous assortment of articles culled from manufacturers, leaving his salesmen to sell what is easiest to sell, or to his customers to select what their uninstructed fancies suggest. Like the taylor, the couturier and the maitre-d'hotel, he must sell something more than 'goods'. He must make himself known as an artist whose rare natural endowments and long years of careful training have fitted him for exceptional service; whose taste, judgement and experience are worth paying for.

Such rhetoric did not accord with the cut-throat practices of many large retail firms, exemplified by Maples.

The firm was established as a furniture shop in Tottenham Court Road in about 1840. In their early years they specialised in mattress making and shifted quantities of what was termed 'low class furniture' to the working classes. Competition from the newly established Co-operative Society furniture stores in the 1870s led them to market better quality goods for the middle classes. Their profits were quickly increased during this period by cutting out the wholesalers and buying direct from the makers. Although some furniture was produced in their own workshops the bulk of the huge range of stock for which they were renowned was obtained by various unscrupulous means from the multitude of small makers in the vicinity and eastwards who prospered and perished at the hands of Horace Regnart, the office boy who became Maples business manager and received a knighthood in 1906 for his services to the furniture industry. When the Select Committee on the Sweating System investigated the furniture trade in 1888 so many witnesses had grievances against Maples that one of the directors, John Blundell Maple, MP was summoned to answer questions. It was standard practice for them to automatically deduct at least 5 per cent from every invoice presented. Payment was often withheld until Saturday afternoons, by which time a small maker was so desperate for cash to pay wages they could be forced to accept an additional charge of anything up to 20 per cent for cashing a cheque. It was also common for Maples to supply materials for which they charged considerably more than the usual market price. When large orders were received by small firms it was often necessary for them to take bigger premises and 'put on' more men. Loans were made available at extortionate rates for such purposes. Every opportunity was taken to squeeze small masters who were in turn expected to squeeze their employees. When one muster, who gave evidence, was asked to make up an order for far less than the estimated price

he was told by Maples buyer to cut his labour costs, which he protested were already as low as possible. The buyer's reply was:

All nonsense; you can get it from the men; you may squeeze it out of them, and those that you cannot squeeze you may shunt; it is just as easy to get men, I find, as it is herrings from Billingsgate.

Many of the practices employed by Maples in the nineteenth century continued well into this century amongst the majority of large retailers whose control of the market was such that manufacturers had no choice but to accept their dictates. Story after story can be told about underhand dealing and slippery buyers. It was not uncommon for payment to be received nine months after delivery or for large orders to be given and then cancellation threatened after delivery of the first batch in order to wring a cheaper unit cost from the maker. Even large scale operations like Lebus were subject to such treatment in the 1930s when they were forced to accept big orders on a sale or return basis. Fierce competition amongst manufacturers has discouraged solidarity so that in isolation none, even the largest, have been able to make a stand against the demands of the retailer.

It is ironic under these circumstances that it was customary for retailers to claim that they made the furniture they sold in their own workshops, sometimes stamping it so. The tradition can be traced back to the eighteenth century at least, when it was considered to be more prestigious to buy furniture from a craftsman-shopkeeper rather than a dealer-shopkeeper. During the 1880s small makers objected to retailers like Maples stamping the goods they bought with their own name because it was thought to disguise the origins of the work, thereby fostering the continuance of the sweating system. When John Blundell Maple was questioned before the Select Committee on the precise meaning of the terms, 'Manufactured for Maple and Co','From Maple and Co' and simply 'Maple and Co', his answer was evasive. Forty years later *The Cabinet Maker* carried an article in which retailers were still being criticised for this practice:

... nine times out of ten he (the retailer) tries to suggest that he makes all the goods that he sells and announces in some prominent place in his shop that he is a 'Cabinet Maker and Upholsterer', whereas he may merely have a repair shop where odds and ends of work can be done. It seems to be a needless fiction that the retailer makes every article he sells. And yet there is a widespread tendency to suggest that the retailer is also a manufacturer.

There is no doubt that it was in the retailers' interests to encourage the belief that the furniture they sold was

"AN EXPLODED IDEA"

IS WHAT THE **VP** SUITE IS NOT!

BUT A PERFECT NOVELTY.

The complete Furniture of a comfortable Bedroom: 3ft. 9in. Wardrobe,
3ft. 6in. Dressing Chest, 3ft. 4in. Washstand, 2 Cane-seat Arm Chairs, Chamber
Service, Bed, Bedding, &c., **FOLDS** into one small case measuring 6ft. by
2ft. 6in. by 2ft. Rigidity and appearance of glued-up Furniture. Patented all
over the World. Write for Illustrated Price List to

The V.P. Folding Bedroom Suite & Furniture Co., Ltd.

Secretary : HORACE W. H. VAUGHAN.   330c, OLD ST., LONDON, E.C.

AGENTS WANTED.

The V.P. Folding Suite & Furniture Co. Ltd., 330c Old Street EC2

*Advertisement in **The Cabinet Maker**, June 1896*

(Greater London Council)

also made by them, because customers would pay more for a name which guaranteed the quality of the product. It also conjured up vague ideas of 'craftsmanship' which carried associations of 'honesty' and nostalgia for a Golden Age, enhancing at the same time the endless reproduction and period styles that were then the dominant fashion.

Unlike many other industries, furniture manufacturers left advertising and marketing to the retailer. Advertising and branding by manufacturers did not develop to any degree until the middle of this century. Whether deliberately fostered by the retailer or not, the anonymity of the manufacturer tended, so far as the public was concerned, to leave the impression that the furniture they bought was made by the retailer. Retailers opposed branding by manufacturers because they considered it would reduce their function to being merely distributors whereas they acquired their reputation by the individuality of the products they bought and their skill in buying them according to the customer's requirements. Branding also involved price fixing which retailers objected to because it meant a fixed margin and the practice was for retailers to fix their own margin to suit the 'special circumstances' of their business. The advantages of branding to the manufacturer were that they could create demand from the public and overcome the conservative attitudes of retailers to innovation and modern design. The retailers' knowledge of the market has been acknowledged by manufacturers for a long time. In 1942 when the Board of Trade met with furniture manufacturers to discuss plans for the Utility furniture scheme, a strong plea was made to involve retailers on the proposed advisory committee, because it was argued that only they knew what the public would accept. In the post-war period the growing design profession had accused retailers of manipulating both the manufacturer and the consumer and preventing the development of new designs. Retailers will always tend to 'play safe', only buying what they know will sell. The adventurous or design conscious manufacturer will consequently have difficulty in finding outlets. The consumer is not therefore given the chance to choose and is obliged to accept only what is made available by the retailer.

In the post-war years the retailers mark up has gradually risen from 33 per cent to over 200 per cent in some instances. The role of mass distribution retailers as a separate financial power has developed rapidly. Volume production and mass distribution have not been adequately integrated with the consequence that manufacturers have lost touch with changing markets which creates difficulties in redirecting and co-ordinating production. Furniture distribution nationally is now concentrated in the hands of a few giant discount retailers led by MFI and Texas. Their buying strategy is based on price discounting. Scores of small firms such as those that characterise the traditional East London industry, have folded through dependence on a single retailer. Others have gone out of business because they have been unable to break exclusive relationships between retailers and a single supplier. Despite the dominance of the giant stores, roughly 25 per cent of the market in 1981 was made up by so-called independent retailers many of whom, especially in the London area, still buy from East London firms.

Export trade

In the eighteenth and early nineteenth century Britain was the largest exporter of furniture in Europe. London was the predominant centre of the trade. In 1830 the total value of 'cabinet and upholstery wares' exported was £55,892 and by 1850 this had almost doubled to £100,000. The overseas market was greatly stimulated by the settlers and officials who populated all parts of the British Empire in ever increasing numbers during the second half of the century.

Some East End manufacturers exploited overseas markets in the Dominions, India, the Colonies, the USA and Argentina. Successive governments from the 1870s to the 1930s promoted the idea of 'complementary economies'; the Empire provided Britain with raw materials and in return purchased manufactured goods.

Because of the complexities of the paperwork involved and the difficulties of transporting furniture, the export trade in the nineteenth century was restricted to large operations or specialist firms. Some big retailers had branches overseas. Maples for example had shops in Paris, Buenos Aires and Montevideo. Other firms worked through agents. Customers could also place orders directly either whilst on trips to London or by means of catalogues. Specialist firms like the V.P. Folding Bedroom Suite & Furniture Co Ltd, 330c Old Street, in 1895 launched patented designs which overcame the problems of packing and haulage. Employing modern machinery, they produced folding furniture said to be indistinguishable from 'glued-up' pieces. As well as packing flat — a 5ft x 7ft sideboard could be folded into a 10 inch package and furthermore, it was better suited to tropical climates since the glues commonly used could not withstand excessive heat and moisture.

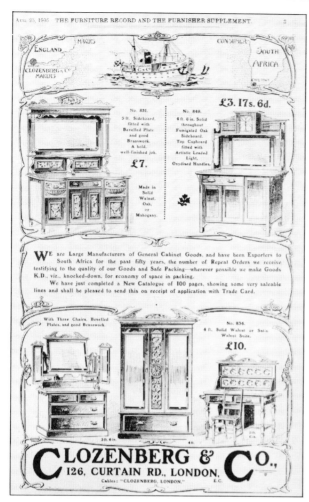

Hille's 'breakfront' bookcase 1946-7
(Hille International Ltd.)

Clozenberg & Co., 126 Curtain Road, London EC2
Advertisement in **The Furniture Record**, 25 August 1905
Clozenberg's specialised in exports to South Africa.
(Photo Studios)

Mr H.E. Richold, a leading South African agent
Photograph in **The Furniture Record**, 25 August 1905
Mr Richold went to South Africa in 1890 as a strolling player. Having then run
his own furnishing business in Cape Town for 10 years, he established himself
as an agent for several big British firms, including E. Atkins and H. Herrmann.
Much travelled, he crossed from England to South Africa 25 times in less than
15 years.
(Photo Studios)

The export trade was disrupted by the First World War. Manufacturers were warned by the trade press of the shortsightedness of neglecting overseas advertising and failing to maintain agents abroad. By the 1920s trade was flourishing again and traditional British furniture was in demand from high-class retailers in Europe, North America and even Japan.

East End firms specialising in quality reproduction work were well placed to exploit this market. In 1927 *The Cabinet Maker* produced a Special Dominions Issue which commented on the use of 'old-fashioned furnishing' in thousands of homes in the Dominions and the USA. An 'English home', it was said, induced visions of an 'ideal state of comfort and well-being'. Some firms, notably Beresford & Hicks, 131-139 Curtain Road, also exported antique furniture. One of the most successful firms in the export trade was S. Hille & Co., 140, Old Street, who had a considerable number of clients in the USA, Australia, Egypt, India and South Africa. In the inter-war years about 15 per cent of their output was exported. After the war Ray Hille's daughter, Rosamind and her husband, Leslie Julius, went on a selling trip to the USA in 1946, where they secured an order for 'breakfront' bookcases, a tall bookcase with a fold-down desk. The success of the trip was such that they were soon making 10 breakfront bookcases a week for export, as well as Adam and Hepplewhite dining room suites and coloured lacquer work furniture.

Since the development of containerisation and 'roll on/roll off' ferries in the 1950s exporting furniture has become much easier. From 1960 to 1980 the value of UK furniture exports rose from 2.5 million to 245 million. Until 1979 Britain had a favourable balance of trade in furniture but since then the balance has moved into ever increasing deficit. Manufacturers of contract furniture such as Lucas Furniture Systems Ltd, Wick Lane, have secured prestigious foreign contracts in recent years with multi-national companies and banks. The mainstay of the market is still sales of reproduction furniture to Europe, the USA and now the Middle East.

Design

Since the early nineteenth century industry has expressed an increasing awareness of 'design' as a marketable commodity. As consumers have little knowledge of how furniture is made and the materials employed in its construction, it follows that purchasing decisions will be based on look — or style. Because furniture, like clothing, is an expression of status and personality, the public demands variety. Individuality was a selling point. 'Specials' became a trade term for extravagant or unusual designs. Singularity was also marketed in the form of 'novelties' which could be bizarre shaped chairs or imaginative types of furniture such as W.H. Vaughan & Co.'s bicycle cabinet for halls.

Stylistically, furniture made in East London can be divided into two main types — modern and reproduction. In the nineteenth century reproduction furniture was produced in a great variety of styles, the Victorians being keen on anything that looked historical or exotic. Designs from every period could be found, often with different names: Gothic, Tudor/Elizabethan, Jacobean, Queen Anne, Chippendale, Hepplewhite, Adam/Adams, Sheraton, Louis XIV, Louis XV and Louis XVI. Although some pieces were direct copies of original designs, the bulk of it was only loosely based on historical styles. The multitude of permutations created inventive, hybrid styles that bore little resemblance to the term applied. Romantic sounding historical names were sometimes given to certain styles as a sales ploy. Modern styles, known at the time as 'Artistic', 'Quaint' or 'Progressive', were also produced in great quantities for a typically younger, middle-class market. Reflecting the concerns of artists/designers of the day, these styles used ideas taken from, in the 1870s-1880s, Japanese and Arab/Moorish art, and in the 1890s-1900s, the continental 'Art Nouveau' style.

The demand for reproduction furniture continued into the twentieth century. Styles were slow to change. Similar types were still to be found with Jacobean, Adams or Sheraton looks being the most popular in the inter-war years. The emphasis in marketing such designs was now on the traditional rather than the historical. The demand for old treasured furniture was such that some dealers stocked antiques alongside reproduction lines whilst certain firms, notably Chippendale Workshops, Hoxton Street, offered customers a 'genuine antique finish' on all their goods for an additional charge of 10 per cent. From the late 1920s modern designs were more popular and also marketed more vigorously than in the preceding period. Almost all manufacturers produced 'Modern' ranges, the style of which would now be termed 'Art Deco'.

Few firms employed designers. In the nineteenth century some large wholesalers used designers on a freelance basis, primarily for illustrating catalogues, such as those produced by Wm. Wallace & Co. Others would occasionally purchase designs by reputable designers like Bruce Talbert and C. F. A. Voysey. It was not until the 1950s that design-con-

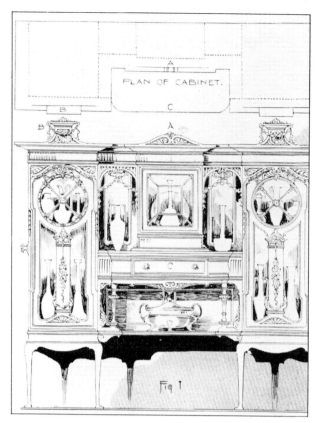

Plan of cabinet
Published in **The Cabinet Maker** 1897
The trade press was an important source for designs.
(Photo Studios)

Hille Chinese Chippendale chairs 1918-1939
This range of lacquer furniture formed a bridge between strict reproduction
styles and the more fanciful forms of Art Deco.
(Hille International Ltd.)

Hille Swan Chairs 1937
Designed by Ray Hille, these chairs typify the extraordinary shapes of the Art
Deco style.
(Hille International Ltd.)

Messrs. W.H. Vaughan & Co., 332-334, Old Street, EC1
Notice about Bicycle Cabinet, **The Cabinet Maker**, November 1897
Novelties such as these were frequently reported in trade notices
(Photo Studios)

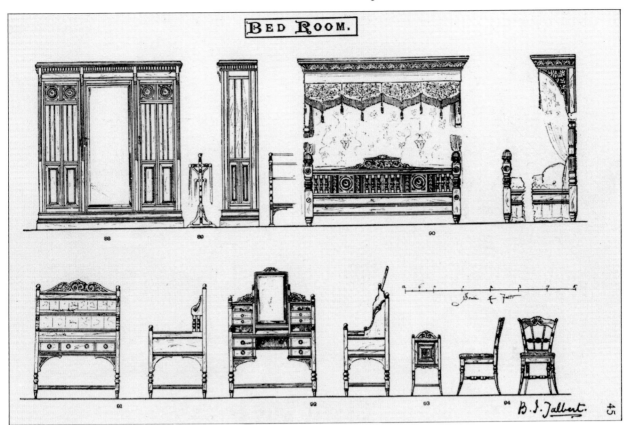

Fashionable Furniture...a Monthly Budget of Designs and Information for the Cabinet, Upholstery and Decoration Trades, a special publication by The Cabinet Maker 1881

Bedroom Furniture designed by Bruce Talbert
The bedhead (no 91) on this sheet was made by Vaughan's.
(British Architectural Library/RIBA)

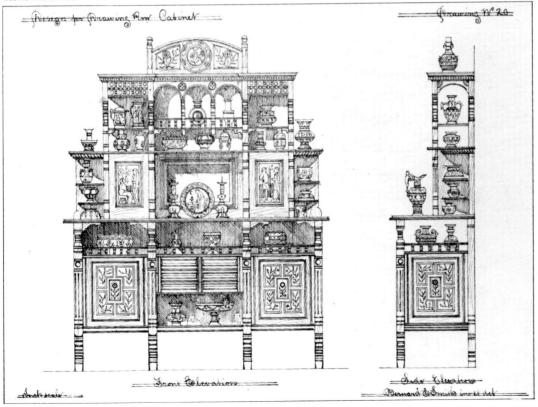

Design for Drawing Room Cabinet
Books such as these were used by some firms as sources of designs.
(British Architectural Library/RIBA)

T. Marigold, 1-2 Knottisford Street, E2
Design for wardrobe 1890s
This is an original design made by a trained draughtsman, whose initials
appear in the bottom right hand corner. It is likely that he was employed to
draw this from a made up piece for showing to prospective clients. Small firms
such as this one were unable to afford the cost of lavishly printed catalogues.
They used instead drawings such as these mounted in card to market their
range.
(Photo Studios)

T. Marigold, 1-2 Knottisford Street, E2
Drawing of a sideboard 1890s
This is a finished but awkward pencil drawing which was probably made by Mr
Marigold himself for a client.
(Photo Studios)

Smarts, 19-25 Oxford Street, W1
Order Form advertising hire purchase plan
(Photo Studios)

J. Collier & Sons Ltd., 134-142, Clapham Road, SW9
Front cover of catalogue 1930s
(Photo Studios)

scious firms took on designers, the most famous of whom was Robin Day, who started working for Hille in 1949. Having been brought up in the furniture-making town of High Wycombe he had trained in a local firm, producing drawings for the shop floor, before winning a scholarship to the Royal College of Art. His strengths as a designer were his great interest in and understanding for materials and production techniques and his involvement in the construction of models and prototypes. Hille supported his experiments which produced many innovative and now 'classic' designs. . Hille were by far the most successful East London firm to employ designers, but there were others that followed a similar course. Doris Young, manager of Evans of London Ltd., Old Ford Road, from 1947 to 1979, encountered some problems with designers who had no experience of the shop floor which created endless practical difficulties and earned them little respect amongst 'the men', who referred to one young designer as a 'long haired git'.

For a great many East End firms, from the nineteenth century to the post-war period, designs were made by the boss or manager, skilled craftsmen who could combine at least elementary draughtsmanship with a detailed knowledge of timber and construction. Some were recognised within the profession, such as Mr J. Beresford of Beresford & Hicks, 131-139, Curtain Road, who was in 1929 described as 'a designer of great distinction... also one of the best-known oarsmen on the Thames'. Nathan Bloom of N. Bloom, 71 Fanshaw Street, partly attributed his success to the fact that he was his own designer; being himself a practical cabinetmaker, he could not merely get out working drawings but also superintend the manufacture in all stages. Some makers never used drawings and worked instead from memory, designing as one old turner described it, 'with your fingers'.

East End furniture was not always made from working drawings or blueprints; it was more usual to work from photographs or pictures culled from a variety of sources. Copying was an accepted practice; it was part of the East End way of working. Numerous publications illustrating designs for furniture and interiors by architects and draughtsmen were produced in the later part of the nineteenth century as aids for furniture makers. Works such as Bernard Smith's *Designs for Furniture in the Neo-Jacobean Style,* published by Batsford in 1876, were clearly intended to inform and educate the makers of 'the Tottenham Court Road style'. Practical notes on materials and construction were included as an additional aid. The trade press provided a cheaper source of ideas in illustrations with reviews of exhibitions and notices of new lines as

well as in specially commissioned drawings by designers like A. Jonquet, W. Timms and W. Scott-Morton. Periodicals such as *The Cabinet Maker* took advantage of the demand for this kind of material in 1881 with its own publication, *Fashionable Furniture* , copies of which were certainly used by East End firms. This collection of designs, which included one hundred by the well-known designer, Bruce Talbert, was described as 'suitable to middle and high-class requirements'. The commercial advantages of such designs were highlighted in the introduction to the book:

The designs can be left to speak for themselves: that they may yield increased business and reliable information to the trades represented is the wish of the compiler and publisher.

As well as making use of these orthodox sources of designs, much 'pirating' took place. In some cases a firm could receive specifications from a middleman, produce a prototype or drawing and then discover that the design had been passed on to another workshop to be made up at a lower price that did not take the planning time into account. An easy way of copying work by other firms was to look at trade catalogues or photographs used by sales representatives. A more skilled task was sometimes carried out by boys, in their lunch break, who were sent up to West End stores, notably Heals, to measure up pieces in the window by eye and to memorise construction details for the boss. Heals were evidently unhappy about pirating. In 1900 *The Cabinet Maker* was refused permission to reproduce a photograph of one of their pieces exhibited at the Paris Exhibition that year. Disapproval of such practices earned East End makers the name of 'Hackney Road copiers'.

Hire purchase

The growth of hire purchase trading, which enabled the trade to iron out seasonal fluctuations to some degree, was one of the most significant factors in the development of the furniture industry this century. Usually associated with the expansion of multiple store retailing in the inter-war years, it came into use at least a century before. Well before the First World War firms like the Hackney Furnishing Company, whose Head Offices and Showrooms were in Mare Street, had a well established 'Equitable System of House-Furnishing' which was vigorously and imaginatively promoted. In 1911 they brought out a booklet written by the Managing Director, Mr A.M. Stewart with the captivating title, *British Homes: Their Making and Furnish-*

'The Easiest of No-Deposit Terms' Bolsoms', 40-44, Strand, WC2. Catalogue 1930 (Photo Studios)

'Don't wait until your ship comes home!' Bolsoms', 40-44, Strand, WC2. Catalogue c.1930 (Photo Studios)

ing. Aping the language of popular home furnishing publications, it played with concepts of comfort and beauty. The opening words read:

> *Is your home a haven of rest? That is what it ought to be. That is what you would like it to be. That is what you can make it. Two things are necessary in the ideal home — comfort and beauty.*

All this could be yours, of course, with the Hackney Furnishing Company's 'Equitable System of House-Furnishing'. Both the poor and the wealthy stood to benefit from it. As the booklet explained:

> *If you are a poor man with only a few rooms you may have as much real comfort in your home and as much of the spirit of beauty as the nobleman in his ancestral halls.*

or in the words of one 'satisfied customer':

> *I could easily pay you cash for this order, but what's the use? You give me no advantage if I pay cash, and why should I disturb my investments when your system enables me to pay you out of income. If I could get lower prices elsewhere by paying cash I would go elsewhere, but your prices are bottom.*

Subscribers to the system were also entitled to free life insurance to the full value of the goods purchased. The booklet included four pages of testimonials from grateful widows such as that from Mrs E. from Limehouse:

> *Many thanks for your kindness to me through the sad loss of my dear husband, as it is a lot off my mind to know that the account is settled, as far as I am left with two little ones really unprovided for, so that your kindness came as a blessing towards us. Thanking you for your courtesy once more...*

Techniques varied from firm to firm. Some shops claimed 'no reference required', though in practice checks had to be made on all potential customers. Others emphasised that only 'small deposits' were needed. The usual procedure was that a preliminary deposit of 10 per cent on the cash price was paid, then interest of 2½ per cent charged on the balance which could be spread over 12, 24 or 36 monthly payments. Hire purchase trading added considerably to the number of staff required to carry out retail businesses; contracts had to be drawn up, accurate records of purchases, payments made and payments due over long periods of time had to be kept. Outside staff were usually employed to collect instalments and to handle the difficult job of retrieving goods in the case of default of payment. The working capital required to trade in this way was considerable. Specialist finance companies emerged to minimise cash flow problems for firms with a sufficiently high turnover. Over-trading on hire purchase resulted in finan-

cial weakness and this led to many amalgamations in the late 1930s and the transfer of control from furnishing firms to finance companies. Without this form of trading to stimulate demand few economies in mass production would have been possible. The increase of hire purchase trading was such that by the late 1920s an estimated 50,000 firms used the system with over six million agreements in force, two million new agreements being signed annually. In some cases over 90 per cent of sales were hire purchase. The integrity of traders became more important than the quality of the goods they sold or the artfulness of the sales techniques they used.

'Easy credit' enabled many people in the inter-war years to furnish their homes in a way they had previously never considered possible. The middle-class was encouraged to use credit facilities to buy 'better quality' furniture. The social stigma attached to hire purchase in its early days that had made some firms advertise delivery in plain vans, had been completely forgotten by the 1950s. *The Cabinet Maker* proclaimed in 1955 that HP had become 'truly acceptable' to the public:

Nowadays the high rate of taxation and high living costs make it difficult even for the middle class to save to any substantial degree, and they have these credit facilities as normal. A point not stressed enough is that the use of hire purchase often enables couples with a certain amount of capital to purchase much better-quality furnishings than would otherwise be possible.

In the late 1950s several reports appeared commenting on the social implications of hire purchase. A booklet published by the National Council for Social Service in 1957, based on a report by the National Citizens Advice Bureau Committee, stated that the two most common causes of problems with HP were the inability of the hirer to relate commitments to household budgets as a whole and high-pressure salesmanship. The worst kind of such selling took place on door steps, particularly in working class districts and on new housing estates. The report recommended the rewording of agreements to make them 'intelligible to ordinary people' and that they be sent through the post to enable hirers to read them carefully before signing. Other proposals included the introduction of standard record cards, prominent display of cash prices alongside HP prices and the use of badges of membership of trade associations. Another document was produced in the same year by the Christian Economic and Social Research Foundation presenting the results of a survey into conditions under which young people were trying to establish homes in London, Birmingham and Leeds. It pointed out that over 60 per

Wm. Wallace & Co., 151-155, Curtain Road, EC2

'The Liverpool Exhibition' Bedroom Suite no. 20

It was usual for firms to produce special ranges for exhibitions.

(Silver Studio Collection)

Daily Mail Ideal Home Exhibition 1968

Waring and Gillow's display of Lebus's Europa range furniture

(Photo Studios)

cent of new families made use of credit facilities and that 'due to various influences, 80 per cent of families with three or more children indulge in HP, over half of them articles of home entertainment, whilst the level of nutrition sinks even lower'. The Government was asked to consider the provision through the Post Office of a means whereby young people could acquire essential domestic equipment at reasonable interest charges 'instead of occasioning those who supply the service to charge more for it'. A correspondent in *The Times* described the suggestion as 'extremely dangerous'.

By the 1960s hire purchase trading was changing as the Government, attempting to control the economy, tried to restrain its use by increasing the size of the minimum down payment and reducing the time span over which payments could be made. With the rise of credit card trading which does not involve repossession of goods on default of payment, the use of hire purchase in furniture retailing is becoming a thing of the past.

Exhibitions

Exhibitions stimulated the interchange of stylistic ideas and were also seen as a means of educating the public in design matters. The late nineteenth century has been described as 'the age of exhibitions'. During this period they represented a major promotional opportunity for firms able to invest the capital outlay required for getting out new designs, display stands, lighting, cleaning, attendants, packing and transport. Exhibitions were organised primarily for manufacturers and wholesalers to attract orders from retail customers. Some exhibitions were trade only, the biggest of which was the Annual Furnishing Trades Exhibition and Market at Olympia, established in 1896; others were aimed specifically at the public. The most famous of these was the Daily Mail Ideal Home Exhibition, first held in 1908. One annual event that always attracted East End firms in particular, because of its proximity to the area, was the Furniture Trade Exhibition held at the Agricultural Halls, Islington (or the 'elephant house' as it was known locally, on account of the circuses that were also held there). Some firms contributed to exhibitions in major regional centres and abroad. Although international exhibitions involved significant resources for minimum returns, other than in terms of reputation, some wholesalers, notably J.S. Henry, 287-297, Old Street, exhibited regularly in this way. East London manufacturers were sometimes selected to represent Britain at overseas fairs, as was the case with Gabe & Pass, Fanshaw

Street, Hoxton, who were invited by the British Institute of Industrial Art in 1925 to exhibit a dining suite in the British section of the International Exhibition of Modern Art in Paris that year. On the whole exhibitions declined in importance and in popularity after the First World War as advertising and other methods of marketing were developed.

Advertising

Unlike other industries, furniture manufacturers have tended to leave advertising to the retailers. By the 1880s advertising appeared separately in department store budgets. Shoolbreds were the first shop reputedly to place a full-page advertisement in *The Times*. Opportunities to advertise increased with the growth of local newspapers, women's magazines and trade journals. Some firms also produced enamel signs for display at railway stations. Less costly than advertising, many West End stores attracted press attention and publicity by announcing the introduction of innovations such as lifts, electricity and cash registers or visits from celebrities such as Lily Langtry and Ellen Terry. Many East End manufacturers placed advertisements in the trade press. In the early days emphasis was placed on giving information about the range of goods produced rather than making claims for the product. Lists of furniture types were often enlivened with fine drawings of premises or pieces of furniture. For retailers, both large and small, local papers offered an excellent means of promotion. *The Hackney Gazette*, published three times a week, carried regular advertisements in the 1920s-30s by multiple stores like Smarts, who produced several new images each year, and local shops such as Jays Furnishing Stores, 223-225, Whitechapel Road, whose advertisements were no less inventive, and McCarthy's, 179-181, Bethnal Green Road. Newspapers such as this one were such an effective medium that even the West End stores like Maples used them to promote one-off events such as sales.

Window display

Shop windows formed the most direct link between retailer and consumer. Window displays gave rise to a great deal of publicity. They were considered more powerful than newspaper advertising. In 1865 Henry Mayhew noted the emphasis on the extravagant use of window dressing in London shops. At first such practices were regarded as vulgar, established firms

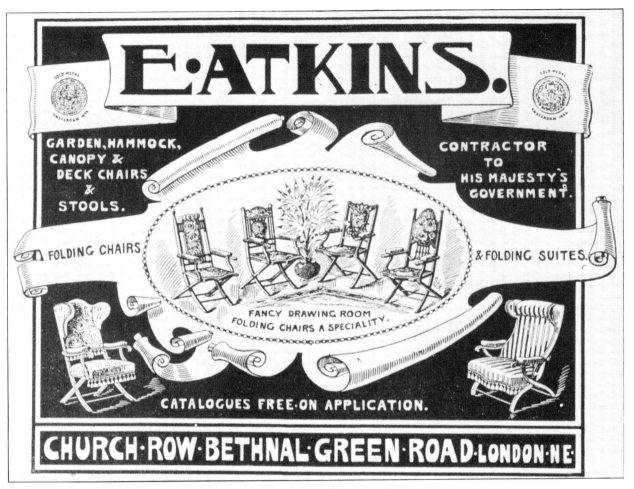

E. Atkins, Church Row, E2
Advertisements in **The Furniture Record**, 27 August 1905
(Photo Studios)

Smart Bros. Ltd., 321, Mare Street, E8
Advertisement in the **Hackney Gazette**, 1 July 1925
Smarts advertised every week in **The Hackney Gazette** throughout the 1920s
and 30s with snappy new copy and images each month. They were the first
furniture firm to draw upon women's magazines, cinema and popular songs as
marketing gimmicks.
(London Borough of Hackney Archives Department)

preferring to rely on their reputation. In 1875 the *Furniture Gazette* reported on different displays to be seen in London shops. Maples and Shoolbreds were described as having:

> ...*magnificent displays in their large well-arranged windows, of resplendent carpets, non-curtain fabrics, and inlaid cabinet work, aiming more at the beautiful in the popular than in the severely high-art sense.*

They relied less on price, as was the case with some of their competitors like Oeztmanns in Hampstead Road, and more on pattern and texture to arrest attention. Older, specialist firms such as Gillows or Jackson and Graham would in contrast make no display at all, 'relying on their superior reputation alone' or show only one piece 'distinguished for some rare excellence or colouring.' Before the First World War multiple stores used the same display methods as other types of retailer, that is, as much stock outside as inside the shop. The impact made by some of these firms in later years is highlighted by a report in *The Cabinet Maker* in July 1937 on Easterns in Croydon whose window display was censored by the police:

> *Easterns, to secure a realistic atmosphere employed a wax model of a girl in bed and a pyjama-clad male figure sitting. But the display attracted such attention and so much comment that the police asked the manager to change it. Now the 'husband' has been moved to another window...*

Catalogues

There is a noticeable difference between catalogues supplied by wholesalers and manufacturers for retail consumption and those provided by retailers or wholesalers who supplied direct to the public. The purpose of the latter was to show not only ranges of stock but also to make furnishing suggestions. Furniture catalogues were used as a means of creating images of ideal homes designed to capture the imagination of the consumer. Some early catalogues were lavishly produced. Shoolbreds, for example, established a reputation for artistic catalogues, good enough to 'grace a drawing room table', which presented artists' impressions of interiors as well as drawings of individual pieces of furniture. These artistic catalogues contrasted with others of the day which showed furniture in stylistically heterogeneous groups rather than in set rooms. As one critic pointed out in the *Furniture Gazette* (May 1874):

> *You might as well take the arms, legs, heads and bodies of a variety of statues, and, jumbling them together in the same way, ask us to pick out the statue we liked*

best, or select a painting from many paintings cut into sections and joined indiscriminately, as to produce such books of designs as our manufacturers of furniture commonly give their customers to furnish and decorate their rooms.

In the inter-war years the development of colour photography facilitated the design of catalogues that copied the style of women's magazines and film magazines. This format was used most imaginatively by multiple stores like Smarts and Bolsoms that had branches in Hackney and Bethnal Green respectively. Smarts, who 'furnished a million homes and won a million hearts', used features on the homes of film stars such as Merle Oberon, Carole Lombard and 'lovely' Jessie Matthews. The furniture was arranged in room sets with one or two figures that echoed the style of black and white movie stills. The models used a stock variety of poses: woman adjusting garter, man tying shoe, woman laying table, man reading newspaper, woman at dressing table decked with flowers, woman sitting at man's feet by the fireside. They even incorporated a short romance called *Honeymoon - A Complete Love Story* by Garth Preston. This format was well-suited to the marketing of modern furniture. It was common for traditional styles of furniture to be shown in interiors which suggested baronial halls rather than suburban 'semis'. Illusions of grandeur were further enhanced by the use of stately names for ranges such as: Buckingham, Beaumont and Clarendon.

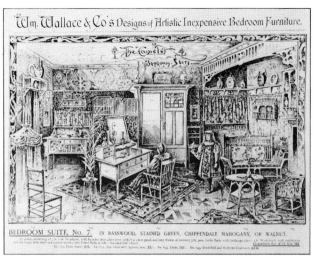

Bolsoms', 40-44, Strand WC2
Catalogue c.1930
(Photo Studios)

Wm. Wallace & Co., 151-155 Curtain Road, EC2
Catalogue c.1895
(Silver Studio Collection)

Smarts, 19-25 Oxford Street, W1
Catalogue c.1935
(Photo Studios)

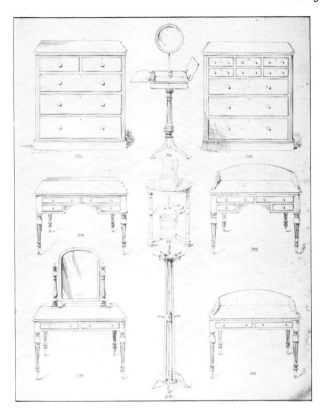

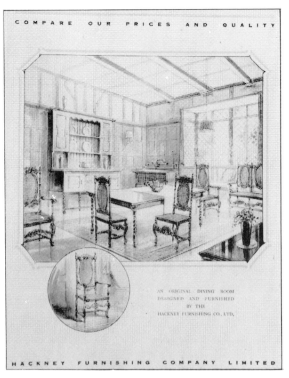

Wm. Walker, 119 Bunhill Row, EC1
Catalogue c.1880
(British Architectural Library/RIBA)

Hackney Furnishing Company Ltd., Mare Street, E8
Catalogue c.1925
(Photo Studios)

Hackney Furnishing Company Ltd., Mare Street, E8
Catalogue c.1900
(Photo Studios)

'A Corner of a Chippendale Interior'
Published in **The Cabinet Maker**, 27 July 1907
(Photo Studios)

Turner & Son, 131, St John Street, Hoxton, N1
Designs for furniture 1880s
(Richard Davis)

Turner & Son, 131, St John Street, Hoxton, N1
Designs for furniture 1880s
(Richard Davis)

'Quaint Furniture for the Bedroom' by H. Pringuer
Published in **The Cabinet Maker**, Coloured Supplement, August 1897
(Photo Studios)

'A Stuart Bedroom Suite'
Published in **The Cabinet Maker**, Coloured Supplement, January 1898
(Photo Studios)

Lusty & Co., Bromley-by-Bow, E3
Catalogue for 'Lloyd Loom' products c.1935
(Photo Studios)

S. Hille & Co., Lea Bridge Road, E10
Formed plywood chair c.1950
(Hille International Ltd.)

Andrew Kindler, 44, Cannon Workshops, West India Dock, E14
Breakfast Table
(Independent Designers Federation)

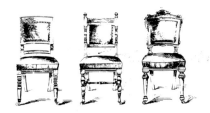

Chapter Three

GETTING ORGANISED:
Trade Unions in East London

Early Days

Upholstery Unions

French Polishers

National Amalgamated Furnishing Trades Association
(NAFTA)

World War I

Women

East End Campaigns

World War II

The National Union of Furniture Trades Operatives
(NUFTO)

This campaign against imported furniture concerned not only the threat to
British workers' employment, but also the exploitation of cheap labour in other
parts of the world.
(FTAT)

GETTING ORGANISED:
Trade Unions in East London

Early Days

Henry Mayhew considered that it was trade union organisation which distinguished the 'honourable' from the 'dishonourable' sectors of the furniture trade. Whilst the division between the West End and East End is usually taken to parallel the 'honourable' / 'dishonourable' split, it is important to understand that there was some trade unionism in the East End before the mid-nineteenth century. The earliest permanent trade societies of London furniture makers were those formed in the West End from the 1760s. Trade union organisation in this skilled sector of the trade was far from easy or complete but the task was infinitely more difficult in the East End. There, in the nineteenth century, sub-contracting, long hours, low wages, the ease of transfer from worker to independent master or small employer, small isolated workshops, the complete collapse of the apprenticeship system, an acute division of labour and the dual threat of youth labour and unemployment militated against any, let alone effective, trade unionism.

The first known furniture trade union in the East End was formed by a group of cabinet makers in about 1833-4, a time of great upsurge in the trade union movement in general. This was probably the same group which, together with East End chair makers, cabinet makers, and carvers and gilders affiliated in 1834 to the Grand National Consolidated Trades Union (GNCTU), which aimed at 'a fair standard of wages by combinations and strikes' and stressed the importance of all members of one craft belonging to a single union. Unity was difficult to achieve, however, particularly in London: the differences between the highly skilled workers of the West End furniture trade and those employed in the East End proved too great for the development of an all-London union, let alone a national one.

During the 1830s and 40s some furniture makers in the East End came to doubt the effectiveness of industrial militancy without political power in terms of benefiting working people. They looked to Chartism with its political programme for parliamentary democracy based on manhood suffrage, to improve their lot. In London by 1840 Chartism had developed into a mass movement with strong links with and roots in the

trade societies. Together with shoemakers and tailors, whose trades were even more seriously threatened by the sweating system, furniture makers played a part in metropolitan Chartism. Those who were most active were those who felt most threatened by low wages, unemployment and displacement by unapprenticed boy labour. East End carvers and chair makers were amongst those who affiliated to the National Association of Trades (NAUT) in the hope that this larger body would overcome the problems faced by small, isolated and, therefore, weak trade unions. At any rate, the NAUT successfully mediated on behalf of a group of members who went on strike in 1847 against their employer, a chair and sofa manufacturer in Tabernacle Row, in the East End.

At the height of activity in London in support of the Charter in 1848, some cabinet makers joined the carvers and chair makers as did some unemployed upholsterers. Chartist agitation was vigorous in East London in 1848, a year of great distress in all the London furniture trades. With employment at about 30 per cent, and with many furniture makers either only in work part of the time or for greatly reduced wages, it is not surprising that East End furniture makers joined tailors, shoemakers and others in the Chartist movement in an attempt to improve their situation.

The failure of Chartism spelled the end of hope for many East End furniture makers. It knocked the stuffing out of those who had been genuinely enthused by radical ideas and/or had hoped for an immediate improvement in their lot. The East End trade societies had not managed to put down very strong roots in the 1830s and some disappeared without trace. It was more than post-Chartism demoralisation, however, which made the task of trade unionism doubly difficult in the 1850s. The intervening decade had witnessed a huge increase in the number of small masters working on their own. This militated against any interest in collective organisation, as did the fact that most of the other workshops remained small and isolated one from another. Hunger and fear of unemployment further worked against organising with fellow workers against the employers.

Alliance Cabinet Makers Association demonstration at Hyde Park 1875
Five members had been imprisoned for peaceful picketing. On their release
there was a mass rally of trade unions. Public opinion was aroused and a long
campaign eventually forced modification of the law.

East End trade unions in 1850

What trade union organisation there was in the East End in 1850 was the highest amongst cabinet makers but there were only 140 union members, as opposed to about 1000 non-members, in the whole of the area (i.e. 12 per cent were unionised). Only 130 out of 1558 East End chairmakers (11 per cent) were unionised and 25 out of 263 East End bedstead makers (9 per cent). In 1850 fancy cabinet makers were 'far less political than they used to be': 'patient, temperate and resigned', they were pre-occupied with scraping a living. Politics seemed a luxury. As one fancy cabinet maker remarked to Henry Mayhew: 'politics sir...what's politics to me, compared to getting my dinner and what's getting my dinner compared to getting food for my children'. None of the fancy cabinet makers who worked in the East End were unionised. Nor were the carvers, of whom there were about 200-300 living and working in and around Bethnal Green, Curtain Road and the Moorfields area. Many of them not only worked in their own rooms but slept under their own bench. They worked long hours for whatever low wages the middlemen offered, there being no established scale of prices by which to work. Their only security came from benefit societies rather than trade societies. If these failed then nothing stood between the furniture maker and hard times.

But what did trade union membership mean in the East End in the mid-nineteenth century? The answer is — very little for many members. Trade societies were unable to control the prices paid for jobs nor impose a minimum rate or wage. What applied in one shop was undercut in another. According to one commentator, the East End Cabinet Makers' Society did little more than ensure that new workers did not undercut rates already agreed in a shop and was unable to guarantee standard prices across shops. What trade societies did do was offer some protection against the effects of unemployment, sickness and loss of tools. Chair makers were compensated for loss of time because of fire as well as having their tools insured. The tools of East End cabinet makers were insured for £25 while the bedstead makers' society offered insurance at optional figures of £12, £18 and £25. Unemployment benefit was one of the most crucial safeguards offered by the trade societies. The East End Cabinet Makers' Society paid out 8s per week to unemployed members. Chair makers received slightly more, but only for a limited period. The bedstead makers' society, however, had been unable to provide its members with unemployment relief for some years before 1850. The chair makers ran a strike pay

scheme (£1 for the first four weeks and 16s thereafter) as did the East End cabinet makers (15s per week) but, once again, the bedstead makers were unable to organise such payments.

The second half of the nineteenth century saw several new developments in trade union organisation in the East End. New groups of workers, such as the french polishers, were organised while others amalgamated to form larger associations. The many problems associated with the sweated system, however, were to prove difficult for any trade union and at no stage, and in no craft, was the percentage of workers unionised very high.

The Alliance Cabinet Makers' Association (ACMA)

The East End Cabinet Makers Society had about 40-50 members in 1861 and was known — at least to employers — as the 'forty thieves'. By 1872, when they joined the Alliance Cabinet Makers Association (ACMA) the 'forty thieves' numbered 66. From its inception in 1865 during an upsurge of trade union militancy in a period of good trade and general prosperity, the ACMA had tried to organise the furniture workers of the East End. Its meetings were held there — at the Alliance Hall, Old Street Road — and some were recruited. By 1868, however, it had lost its base amongst these workers and was forced to concentrate on those working in better quality shops in the Tottenham Court Road area. Nevertheless, the ACMA never lost sight of its original objectives and its policy of amalgamations with other societies went some way towards helping it to achieve those ends. The merger of 1872 brought the main body of organised East London cabinet makers into the ranks of the ACMA and others followed. Some of the 91 fancy cabinet makers who joined in 1872 worked in East London as did many of the 80 members of the London Society of Continental Cabinet Makers (mostly German immigrants) who joined the ACMA in 1873. They formed the London No.3 and No.4 branches respectively.

The encompassing of less skilled East End workers led the Alliance to vary its weekly subscriptions (from 7d to 4d per week) to take account of members' wage differentials. However, even the 4d subscription was sufficiently high to ensure the respectability of the East End membership — as well as the solidity of union funds. The range of benefits was basic. Death benefits to help meet funeral expenses came in the form of 'gifts' estimated according to length of membership. The sick fund was financed out of voluntary payments and tools were insured on a sliding scale. Unemploy-

Alex Gossip, General Secretary of NAFTA, addressing Hunger Marchers' rally,
Hyde Park, 1934
(FTAT)

ment benefit ranged from 8s per week (for those who paid a 4d subscription) to 14s.

For all members, but particularly those in the East End, the buffer against the effects of unemployment was extremely important. Some years were worse than others in a trade that suffered regular seasonal fluctuations: in 1897, for instance, the ACMA paid out over £800 in unemployment benefits in a year of severe crisis in the furniture trade. So acute was the situation that the Alliance produced an extensive list of London workshops where its members might find work. The list, which ran to more than 20 pages, included 50 cabinet making workshops in the East district (Bethnal Green and Hackney) and 65 in the East-Central district (from the City to Curtain Road); 13 fancy cabinet making shops in the East district and 23 in East Central; 36 chairmaking establishments in the East district and 23 in East Central and 5 cabinet carving shops in the East district together with 20 in East Central. Also specified were 10 establishments which specialised in shop-fitting, an area of work taken up by many furniture makers when they found themselves out of work.

Jewish unions

The Alliance became the largest East End furniture trade union. By the late 1880s and early 1890s it had about 346 members. When the Hebrew Cabinet Makers' Society amalgamated with it in 1889, 200 new members were brought in. The ACMA rules were translated into Hebrew at a cost of 5 gns and the union paid £7 10s 0d for 1000 printed copies. Individual Jewish furniture makers had joined the Alliance before this time but the merger of these two sizeable bodies was an important step in overcoming the segregation, in trade union terms, of Jewish workers.

But not all Jewish workers felt comfortable in the new association, despite the fact that some of the ACMA branches were now heavily dominated by Jewish workers. Some also objected to the union's campaign against piece work and broke away to form the Independent Hebrew Society in 1895. Sensitive to the need to prove its usefulness to Jewish workers, the ACMA emphasised the benefits it had brought them, claiming in 1895 that:

Our Hebrew members have been rescued from the grip of the sweater and placed under the same conditions enjoyed by their fellow members of British and other nationalities.

This came after a four week withdrawal of labour in 'Hebrew shops' which forced those particular employers to agree to the new wage rates (a minimum of 9½d per hour), fixed overtime rates and a 52½ hour week which the Employers' Federation had agreed with the ACMA. Such claims about rescuing workers from the grip of the sweaters proved over optimistic as great numbers of furniture workers, both Gentile and Jew, remained victims of the East End system well into the twentieth century.

'the best representatives of the trade'

Despite the weakness of trade union organisation in the East End in general and possibly because of the many difficulties involved in such activities, the Booth report considered the most active trade unionists in the area to be:

among the best representatives of the trade ... good craftsmen ... who are also conscious of the importance of maintaining and extending the principle and practice of association. The work that these men are doing ... in the face of great difficulties, and against tendencies that are as powerful as they are antagonistic, is one of the bright spots in this group of trades, for it is one in which action is guided by some recognition of a community of interest, and by concern for the welfare not only of one or a few, and not only of a trade society, but also of those who from ignorance, selfishness, inefficiency, poverty, or from some other cause are still without its borders.

Anti-fascist demonstration in the East End 1930

Members of the East End United branch were active in the anti-fascist

movement.

(FTAT)

Upholstery Unions

There was little or no trade union organisation amongst East End upholsterers until the late 1880s. Unsuccessful attempts to unionise these workers had been made in the 1860s and 70s but it was not until the huge growth of trade unions for unskilled workers after the great dock strike of 1889 that new moves were made. The old West End Upholsterers Society (which dates back at least to the early nineteenth century) insisted on a full craft training for all its members, thereby excluding virtually all those who worked in the East End. Although this society eased its entry requirements in the late 1880s, it did so too late because a separate society to cater for the needs of East End workers was formed in 1889. This met regularly at the 'Horse and Groom' in Curtain Road, right in the heart of the furniture making area. Within three years its 225 members merged with the newly formed national union of upholsterers, the Amalgamated Union of Upholsterers (AUU), and became known as the London No.1 branch. John Caplin who led the East End Upholsterers' Society into the AUU became its President in 1894.

Another East End branch (No.5) was formed in 1897. This comprised mainly Jewish workers who were employed in shops where the very cheapest class of work was carried on. In order to recruit to this branch and, indeed, to retain membership, the union put out circulars which were part Yiddish/part English for the better understanding of those Jewish members who had difficulty in reading English.

The strength of the AUU, its founders believed, would come from a union which represented all members of the upholstery craft. They viewed with suspicion, therefore, the recruitment of upholsterers by the ACMA and there was some conflict between the two associations. At an official level the ACMA was hostile to the AUU but in many localities the respective branches of the two unions enjoyed good relations.

Nowhere did the new union put more effort and resources than East London. A combination of determination and militant tactics seemed to pay off: the General Secretary of the Union, Lewis Leckie (1897-1923) recalled:

...the method of warfare adopted there, described as guerilla, was very effective and probably the only way to success, considering the vastness of the problem... At the time of the inception of the AUU the East End of London was honeycombed with numerous small employers who viewed the growth of trade unionism with apprehension, and threatened their employees with dismissal if they became members of the union. The men joined up in spite of those threats. Many of the employers worked from hand to mouth, and were little, if any, better off than the men whom they employed. Payment of wages at the end of a week, or when the job had been completed, was not a certainty, and the employers' cheques were often cashed at public houses after banking hours, with no guarantee that the bank account was in good standing.

The enthusiasm of union officials was enormous and, by means of dealing with one workshop after another, they succeeded in gradually improving conditions. Leckie continued:

The method of dealing with the worst employers, from the point of view of the Society, and the efforts to improve working conditions in the workshops concerned, occasionally involved the withdrawal of the men. This caused a certain amount of excitement which both advertised the work of the Society, and had its effects on other employers who recognised its activity, and who became more amenable when their turn came ... The Branch met with considerable success in its own neighbourhood and went on to undertake the further organisation of the men, hitherto unattached, in the district lying towards the West End.

The excessive use of boy labour and piece rates were issues the union was forced to confront in the East End. It was not without some success with regard to the former. The number of apprentices taken in any workshop was often excessively high in relation to adult workers. Some employers were keen to take on young lads as cheap labour; others were concerned only for the premium paid by parents or guardians. From about 1894 the AUU made considerable efforts to convince employers to concede to the rule of one apprentice to three journeymen and a survey taken two years later revealed that in the East End district this average had been attained — indeed, it was slightly below this figure. At first sight this seems a remarkable achievement by the union. However, this low ratio of boy labour to adult labour probably reflects the fact that many firms simply by-passed the apprenticeship system completely, preferring instead to take on 'improvers', i.e. young lads who worked for a low wage while picking up the rudiments of the job. The union was fairly powerless when it came to the crucial question of piece work in the East End. In the late 1890s the AUU Executive could do little beyond piously hope for the elimination of piece work by raising the standard of timed work (the minimum rate in the East End in 1897 was 10d per hour, with 1s per hour as the standard rate). The acceptance by the upholsterers' union of piece rates caused difficulties between it and the cabinet makers' union in later years.

Another aspect of the East End trade which the AUU tackled was that of the wholesale manufacturers. In 1913 the East End members mounted a huge campaign in response to recent developments which had been eroding their standard of living. Once again the story is recounted by General Secretary Leckie:

Reduction in prices or speeding up on task work had gradually tended to bring the standard of living down to rather low a level. Demands were made to the Employers' Federation for one penny per hour increase on time work; ten per cent on piece work; and the reduction of workshop hours to fifty-two and a half per week, not more than one apprentice to three journeymen employed. The requests met with a blank refusal. The men ceased work on July 10. St James' Parish Church Rooms, Curtain Road, Shoreditch, became a very active centre for the six weeks period of the dispute; the rector of the parish (a scion of the aristocracy) having granted its use. He also showed great sympathy with the aspirations of the Union in this effort to raise its standard.

The Employers Association stood firm but so did the upholsterers who, after six weeks of struggle, were victorious.

The announcement that the strike was at an end was made last night at the Shoreditch Town Hall amid a scene of enthusiasm unparalleled in the industrial history of the borough ... Fully 1,000 men were present at last night's meeting, and when it was announced that, as a direct result of the strike, over 700 men had joined the Union, there was a tremendous outburst of cheering.

Mr Leckie (the General Secretary) pointed out that although London had dropped the curtain on its own trouble in Curtain Road, the curtain was only beginning to rise in other parts of the country.

Upholsteresses

It was not until the twentieth century that the AUU turned its attention to organising women workers in the trade. The first attempts at organising upholsteresses in London were made in the 1870s as a result of the activities of the Women's Trade Union League but these were confined to the skilled craftswomen of the West End shops. The Women's Trade Union Association (1889) was launched to organise the less skilled workers of the East End. This association was founded in the wake of the Great Dock strike and the mass organising of unskilled workers. Like so many of the unions founded then, it too faltered — finally collapsing in 1894. Ben Tillet, the famous dockers' leader, knew only too well how difficult it was to organise London's unskilled workers: 'London is the ever great problem ... the Sphinx of Labour'. In hard pressed times, other notable trade unionists regarded women as the Sphinx: Will Thorne claimed that 'Women do not make good trade unionists', while John Burns argued that unions should concentrate on male workers and campaigned to ban married women from employment in order to ease the competition on jobs.

The AUU was exclusively concerned with the rights of male workers until the upholsteresses of the National Federation of Women Workers joined in 1914. Indeed, it actively opposed female employment on certain occasions. In 1904, for instance, the AUU took swift measures to nip in the bud a move by H.M. Dockyard Authorities to employ upholsteresses. The AUU believed this development was taken 'more from ignorance than from any intention of sweating, or from any desire to disturb the status quo'. It was soon dropped and members informed that 'the interests of the trade [were] assured.'

The threat of cheap labour was the great articulated fear of male upholsterers (the inarticulated fears concerning notions of their masculinity were also important — not least because they were unspoken and based on a general prejudice against women). This threat was undoubtedly true as things stood. The solution of improved wages and conditions for women, was only taken up outside the AUU before 1914. It was the National Federation of Women Workers which organised the London upholsteresses, who formed a branch of the Federation in 1910. The AUU paternalistically 'took a kindly interest in it' and amalgamation came in 1914, just in time for the great change in women's work during World War I. It was AUU policy that both men and women working in the upholstery trade should be members of the same union but this did not mean that there was any idea of equal pay for work of equal value or fair promotion opportunities within the union at that time. It should be pointed out, however, that the AUU was no better and no worse than most other unions on these issues, which were not generally taken up in the trade union movement until the 1970s.

Shoreditch Technical Institute: wooodworking class for women 1913
Women were traditionally trained in polishing and upholstery. Many would
have been taught at home. The college also ran courses in machining and
dress-making for the textile trade.
(Greater London Photographs Library)

French Polishers

...The portly stomached magnate of cheap made cabinets Ye slaves of the Rubber who are easily caught in his net. Your days, your nights are his, your children, wives, Blood, sweat and breath are his — your very lives...

(Quoted in F. Herva, *French Polishers and their industry*, 1897 p.83)

The french polishers were mainly organised by two societies founded in 1853 — the Metropolitan French Polishers' Society which organised West End workers and the East End Operative French Polishers' Society. These two societies continued the 'uneven tenor of their respective ways' until 1876 when the East End branch initiated a strike for 8d per hour (1d below the West End rate). The action was backed by the West End society but its failure almost led to the demise of both societies. Within two years the Alliance French Polishers' Society was founded but it did not merge with the East End French Polishers' Society until 1894 when the Amalgamated Society of French Polishers (ASFP) was formed. By this time the ACMA had also begun to organise polishers and the ASFP approached the former for discussions about polishers within that union. There was no resolution to the problem — that came only in 1911 when ASFP amalgamated with the old Alliance Association in what was, by then, NAFTA. Another society established in the nineteenth century, the United French Polishers' Society, which had members in the East End, remained aloof from NAFTA and its successor NUFTO until 1969.

Microcell Strike, late 1950s
This Curtain Road firm which had specialised in aircraft seating made workers
redundant when the Ministry of Defence withdrew its contract in the late 1950s.
(FTAT)

National Amalgamated Furnishing Trades Association (NAFTA)

The Alliance policy of amalgamation continued and in 1902 it joined with the Scottish United Cabinet Makers and Chair Makers Association to form NAFTA. The only sizeable London unions to join the new body in the years before World War I were those of the french polishers. The London Society of French Polishers joined in 1908 and the larger Amalgamated Society of French Polishers three years later.

The french polishers enjoyed a certain reputation as radicals and their decision to join NAFTA may have been influenced by its militant stance on many issues under the leadership of its General Secretary, Alex Gossip. It is difficult, however, to say how far this militant image and union support for socialist and internationalist causes affected the majority of East End members. At one polarity there were, no doubt, those who ignored the leadership's radical gestures so long as the trade union officials did their job well on day-to-day bread and butter issues. At the opposite extreme, there were members who were certainly as radical as Gossip and the Executive Committee. Many of the Jewish immigrants, for instance, brought with them a more internationalist outlook as well as a commitment to radical ideas and politics. They and their children provided the East End's Trade Union movement with some of its doughtiest fighters.

J O'Grady MP

Such members wholeheartedly supported the demand for direct labour representation in Parliament in order to redress anti-trade union legislation. One particular East End furniture maker, who was active in the ACMA gained some degree of celebrity when he became a trade union sponsored MP in 1906. By that time the ACMA had merged with the main Scottish furniture trade union to form the National Amalgamated Furnishing Trades Association. NAFTA was asked by the Labour Representation Committee to nominate a parliamentary candidate and O'Grady was the choice. He went forward with strong radical credentials but disappointed some of his more left-wing supporters, particularly over his support for conscription in 1914.

The right to work

The need and right to work was the main issue emphasised by NAFTA — an issue which touched a chord in every East End worker. With 11 per cent of the national membership out of work in 1908, Alex Gossip focused attention on the injustices of the 'miserable soul destroying system' under which his members were forced to work. He did this by pointing to the fortune of over £2 million left by the recently deceased Sir Blundell Maple, Head of Maple & Co. Much of Maples fortune had, of course, been made by East End workers who supplied the furniture sold in the firm's Tottenham Court Road store.

Despite constant efforts to improve conditions in the East End, the area remained notoriously difficult to organise. Some slight advances were made in isolated shops, but with the outbreak of war in August 1914, other issues took priority. The organising of the East End was shelved — but not forgotten.

ON A 'PLANE' BY ITSELF

'CROID'

'The GLUE with the GRIP'

'Croid' Liquid Glue is the most efficient for all work where a perfect joint and a clean finish are essential. It grips with a tenacity unequalled by any other glue. 'Croid' is rapidly superseding old-fashioned hot glues for all purposes, and has the unanimous approval of leading joiners and wood-workers everywhere.

USED COLD

Approved by H.M. Aeronautical Inspection Department for Aeroplane and Seaplane Construction.

CONVINCING PROOF.

"I enclose order for further half ton of 'CROID' Glue. I have used this glue for over twelve months, and am pleased to say it answers for my work (general wood-working) *better than the best hot glue.*"

INVESTIGATE THE

WORLD'S

STRONGEST

GLUE.

The
IMPROVED LIQUID GLUES
Co., Ltd.,
Gt. Hermitage Street, London, E.

Contractors to H.M. Government.

'Croid': 'The Glue with the Grip'
Advertisement in **The Cabinet Maker**, 30 September 1917
Materials developed during the war for aircraft manufacture hastened
technological advances in the inter-war years.
(Photo Studios)

World War I

Furniture makers rushed to fight for their country. No other union had so high a percentage of volunteers (33 per cent) as did NAFTA. By 1916 4,282 furniture makers had joined up. Many of these came from the East End; from every craft and from every ethnic group within the trade, Many did not return : nine members of the East Central (No.1) branch of the United French Polishers' Society alone were killed in the war. Conscription affected only about 400 furniture makers because those eligible moved into reserved occupations, mainly in aircraft and munitions, while those too old for conscription (by the end of the war the upper age limited had reached 50) were mainly employed at traditional furniture making jobs. The skills of machinists, cabinet makers, chair makers, and carvers were all utilised on the construction of the wooden aeroplanes used in World War I, while upholsterers and upholsteresses covered the body and wings of the aircraft in doped linen.

Joint Industrial Council (JIC)

In December 1918 a Joint Industrial Council for the Furniture Industry, comprising both employers and the main trade unions, was established to regulate and oversee wages, hours, production, grievance procedures, health and safety and education. NAFTA argued for a 44 hour week but the employers would only concede 47 hours — a figure which must have seemed something of a miracle to those East Enders who remembered the long hours of pre-war days. A national ban on overtime was imposed in an attempt to force employers to absorb the large number of ex-servicemen looking for jobs.

Lebus's: group of workers pre 1914
When the firm moved in 1903 they employed over 1,000 furniture workers and
45 office staff.
(Vestry House Museum)

Women

The great fear of the West End furniture makers was always the dilution of their craft by their less skilled colleagues in the East End who were prepared to accept low wages and poor working conditions. During the war both these groups found themselves worried about dilution, firstly by Belgian refugees and then by women workers. As early as December 1914 Gossip warned his members of the dangers of employers treating Belgian refugees not as guests but as cheap labour and NAFTA sent reports to the War Office proving that 'several of the most notorious sweaters in the East End' who were engaged in government work were using Belgian Labour.

On women working in the industry, the official union view was as follows:

We must act with caution, in the interests of our men, in the interest of the nation, and also in the interests of women, to prevent the sweaters of our trade using the war period, and the plea of patriotism to further their own ulterior motives to secure cheap female labour, to the detriment of the trade, the men employed in it, and the thousands of our members fighting their country's battles in all parts of the world. One doesn't want these men to come back and find their places taken by women at one-half of the rate. Innovation may be necessary; women may have to be employed; but to secure proper safeguards is a duty imposed on us all.

The AUU was equally cautious. Many more women joined the union as they increasingly saw the need for trade union organisation. Several advances in wages were made up and down the country by upholsteresses but at least one such request made by the London branches of the AUU was turned down by the employers on the grounds that the union did not contain a sufficient number of upholsteresses to be able to claim to represent them. This rebuff, together with the national agreement of 1916, was just what was needed to spur on the AUU on the question of the recruitment of women. The national agreement fixed women's rates at two thirds of the male rate for comparable work and also stipulated that women working in furniture making should belong to an appropriate trade union.

Both NAFTA and the AUU benefitted considerably.

Furthermore, until 1914 women had mainly worked in polishing and upholstery but during World War I they worked at cutting and preparing wood as well as at packing and labouring. Some also drove the horse-drawn vans and carts in which furniture was moved from shop to shop and finally delivered to the customer. Consequently, NAFTA was forced to change its rules to allow women working at such jobs into union membership — albeit 'emergency membership' for the duration of the war only. By the end of the war, the union as a whole had 3,000 women in membership but there are no separate figures for the East End.

Although certain employers had noted the economic advantage of exploiting women's cheap labour, they did not push this idea after the war. At one level the employers had a forceful union to deal with and it would also have seemed unpatriotic and uncaring to deny work to ex-soldiers — but it went deeper than that. The dominant ideology relating to women and work, particularly ideas about women's inability to handle demanding physical work, such as still pertained in furniture workshops and factories, together with traditional notions of what was 'mens' work' and what was 'womens' work', was so strong that it overrode any consideration of economic advantage. The furniture employers never seriously tried to keep women at the jobs they had occupied during the war. Most women also accepted their experiences in wartime as 'exceptional' and either left the industry or returned to their old jobs without giving voice to any protest. Another consideration was that employers needed to move back to furniture making proper, to the type of production they had left off in 1914. What women had learned in the war were a few furniture making skills applied to aircraft or munitions production. While men with all the necessary skills and knowledge of the various production processes of the trade as practised in 1914 were returning in droves, there was little or no incentive for employers to retrain women. By 1924 only 4 per cent of NAFTA members were women.

Those women who remained in the trade worked mainly in upholstery and french polishing. One of the unions representing male workers in the latter trade, however, resolved in 1919 to vigorously oppose women's 'intrusion into our shops, and to voice our resentment against their organisation'. This policy adopted by the United French Polishers' Society was clearly sexist but it was argued in terms of women being cheap labour and cheap labour bringing down the trade as a whole. The society could, of course, have argued and fought for better pay and conditions for female polishers but instead it chose to actively block their entry into the trade. In 1925 matters came to a head when the United French Polishers' Society

refused to sit on the French Polishers' Federated Committee (the joint committee representing all unions with polishers in membership) so long as NAFTA sent a woman delegate. The latter organisation stood by its decision to have a woman represent their largely female membership in that craft. The UFPS replied by refusing to sit with what it called 'the representatives of cheap labour, be it male cheap labour or female cheap labour'. This was one of the issues which kept the two societies from amalgamating until 1969.

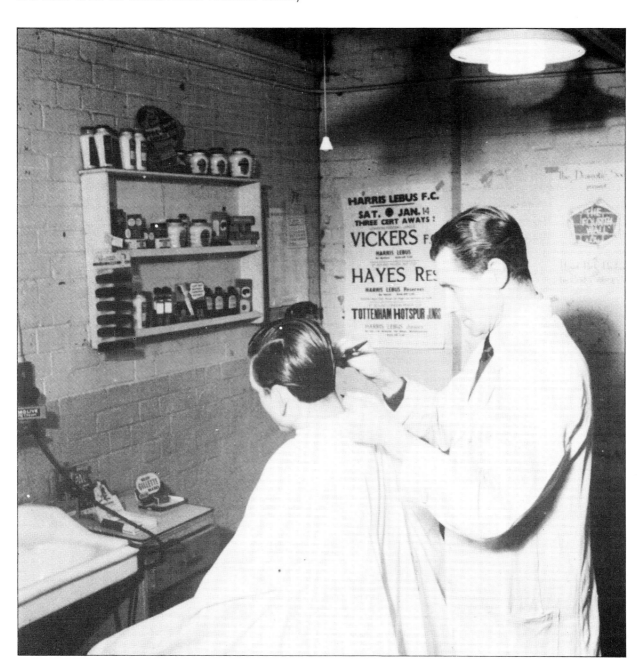

Lebus's, Ferry Lane, N18: barbers shop 1950s
Lebus's resistance to unionisation was coupled with a strong paternalist attitude
towards their workforce, which provided facilities such as these.
(Vestry House Museum)

East End Campaigns

The fundamental problems of the East End trade were not forgotten during World War I. Indeed, Fred Bramley, one of the NAFTA officials with responsibility for the area, wrote movingly and determinedly of the situation there :

> Perhaps some time we shall have our men on strike for sanitary conditions in the workshop, for more air, more light, and the opportunity of being able to breathe whilst getting a living. After the war we shall have to do something big in the East End of London. A revolution in the furniture trade is needed. The sweater must be driven out. Our industry needs purifying. The comparatively decent employer suffers, our men and women suffer, and the community is left to deal with the evil effects of a bad system.

This work became a priority after the war with the establishment of an East End organising branch. The extension of the East End trade into Tottenham was acknowledged by the establishment of a NAFTA branch there in 1918 followed by one in Edmonton in 1929. For all three branches, the inter-war years were extremely active ones.

One of the first steps in the campaign to improve conditions in the East End was the amalgamation in 1918 between NAFTA and the United Furnishing Trades Union — sometimes referred to as the Independent Hebrew Society, under its General Secretary, Jack Cohen. Two other societies joined at the same time: the London Perseverance Cabinet Makers Society and what was probably the last in a long line of societies which called themselves the East End Cabinet Makers' Society. This newly strengthened NAFTA had some successes in the East End in the inter-war years but it proved difficult to make headway with some of the large firms which were developing at that time. The crusade within all firms — large and small — centred on union recognition and the abolition of the payment by results scheme (or PBR as it was known) in favour of day rates. Unfortunately, the upholsterers had long worked to piece rates or payment by results and their trade union, the AUU did not support NAFTA on this particular issue.

Meredew and Lebus

Meredew was the centre of an intermittent struggle over hours and union recognition between 1920 and 1925. Ironically, in the end, it was the Employers' Federation rather than the union which forced Meredew management to cut its weekly hours from 54½ to the 47 in the JIC agreement. NAFTA, however, remained unable to obtain recognition in that particular factory.

With Lebus, the union once again fought hard but, in the end, suffered a major defeat. It may have been the largest furniture factory in the country, but trade unionists reckoned Lebus to be 'as bad as the worst in this country' for working conditions. The issues were payment by results (PBR) and union recognition. Lebus had worked to a PBR system before World War I but from 1914 to 1922 had paid day work rates. In the latter year, however, management determined to return to PBR because:

Restriction of output has been so appalling in all departments that we have come to the conclusion that the only way in which we can carry on business is by introducing a system of payment by results or piece work.

Forced with an ultimatum of accepting piece work or finding work elsewhere, 600 cabinet makers withdrew their labour. However, they were but a small minority in a workforce of 3,500 and the upholsterers did not support them. Furthermore, such was the unemployment in the Tottenham area that Lebus were inundated with applications for the 600 jobs. This defeat did not soften NAFTA's resolve vis-à-vis London's largest employer but it was not until 1939, when war work contracts forced employers to accept trade union representation, that Lebus was unionised.

East End branch, No.15 (NAFTA)

A great deal of the NAFTA organising activity centred around the No.15 branch which included many Jewish members. It met in Brick Lane where, further along the street, was the firm of Fineman and Son. While one Fineman son was an employer, the other was a union district organiser in charge of the No.15 branch. The latter's credentials included the fact that he not only knew the trade well but also spoke Yiddish. One member recalled that the meetings tended to get 'out of hand as they were conducted in a jargon of two or three languages now known as Yinglish'. The branch was well known for its social activities — from its sports club to camping holidays in Devon — and also for its left wing views. Many members of this branch were staunch anti-fascists and played an active part in opposing the Mosleyites in the East End in the 1930s.

Employers, on the other hand, were prepared to use Mosley's black shirts to break strikes. Jack Moss, a union organiser in the post-war period, recounted how, in 1938, one employer employed fascists at 2s 6d per hour when the union rate was 1s 9d per hour in order to break a strike. He also still savours the pleasure he had in organising that shop after World War II. Many of the young Jewish furniture makers joined the Communist Party which they saw as the main opponent of fascism. Indeed, some of the Jewish furniture makers recently interviewed recalled that they only took up trade union activity seriously once they were members of the Communist Party. In other words, their route to militancy in the trade union movement came through their anti-fascist activities. But such activities were not confined to No.15 branch. Throughout the East End anti-fascism was a leading issue and NAFTA nationally was in the forefront of trade union activity on the issue, with Alex Gossip one of the first British trade union leaders to point out the fascist threat. The NAFTA membership responded marvellously to the Spanish Civil War; seven men from the No.15 branch volunteered to fight and, in all, about 35 - 40 NAFTA members joined the International Brigade. Many more were to fight and die in World War II.

Branch meeting, Gravel Pit Hall, Morning Lane, E8 c.1952
The employers' association, the London Furniture Manufacturers Association
was well-organised. This meeting was to discuss action against their decision
to take away a cost of living sliding scale.
(Jack Moss)

World War II

The high point of trade union organisation in the furniture industry came during and in the years immediately after World War II. The Board of Trade sought reputable firms to manufacture Utility furniture and trade union organisers had to approve the firms. Approved firms became closed shops although, as Hew Reid points out in his history of furniture making trade unions, there was, in fact, no compulsion about this. What mattered was that most employers assumed there was or, at any rate, did not want to get on the wrong side of the union. As Jock Shanley, then General Secretary of the AUU relates:

As soon as we knew the name of a factory which was to produce furniture under the utility scheme we sent an official down to meet the management, and told them, 'We have come to sign up all your work people as you are going on to the utility scheme.' The suggestion was that it was a condition of the contract that all workers should be in the union. No one ever questioned it and we established our influence over the whole of the utility making factories very quickly.

The war meant full employment and a decent wage. In 1940 a sliding scale of wages related to a cost of living index was adopted, offering security to a workforce which remembered pre-war unemployment.

Women

Women's rates were two-thirds of the male rate and by 1944 there were 9,286 female members of NAFTA out of a total workforce of 36,707, i.e. approximately one female worker for every four male workers. The women did all furniture making jobs with the exception of saw milling but, just as after World War I, went back to their traditional jobs when the war ended. However, the proportion of women in union membership in the 1950s was about 15 per cent as opposed to only 5 per cent before the war. More recently the percentage of women workers in the trade has fallen and it is difficult to imagine this changing given the rapid decline of the industry.

Women from Lebus's on march against reduction in cost of living allowance
1952
(Jack Moss)

NUFTO Hall, Jockeys Fields, WC2 1954
The hall was opened on 13 November 1954 by Clement Attlee.
(FTAT)

Spiralynx Bedding Works 1975
This firm, notorious for bad employment practices, was the centre of the main
campaigns of the mid 1970s.
(FTAT)

The National Union of Furniture Trades Operatives (NUFTO)

NAFTA concentrated much of its efforts in the post war years on the larger firms, many of which had moved out of the inner East End by the 1950s. In May 1947, NAFTA (46,522 members) joined with the AUU (10,608 members) to form the National Union of Furniture Trades Operatives (NUFTO). In industrial relations the years 1948-1972 (when FTAT, the Furniture Timber and Allied Trades Union was formed) were ones of relative peace. As production rose in the 1950s furniture makers felt entitled to better wages. Indeed, the trade went from being relatively poorly paid before World War II to becoming one of the better paid occupations. However, the general prosperity of the 1950s and 1960s was offset in the furniture trade, by variations in credit restrictions which, because most furniture was by then bought on hire purchase, was a destabilising factor which caused considerable swings in production. At one moment of crisis for the employers in 1952 a wage freeze was threatened, as was the cost of living index. 7,000 furniture workers stopped work in response and an enormous demonstration in London forced the employers to change their minds. In 1960 the 42 hour week was achieved after a five day ban on overtime while the 40 hour week won five years later was achieved without any industrial militancy. In general, most workers, including those in East London felt they were doing fairly well in those years.

Trade unionism in East London changed as the nature of the trade changed. There was less overt exploitation as the very worst of the sweated shops disappeared. Some of the smallish and middling size firms which provided the backbone of the post-war trade had been organised before the war and remained so. Others were never unionised as NUFTO concentrated on the problems faced by furniture workers in the large factories utilising machine mass production. Conditions in East End firms, then and now, varied from the very best traditions of benevolent paternalism to outright cynical exploitation. Today, in times of economic uncertainty, it is not uncommon for workers to identify with their firm and its particular future rather than with the wider interests of the trade union movement. Attempts have been made to offset the decline of traditional manufacturing industries in East London by establishing small workshops or factories. This raises problems for trade union organisation, however, particularly when those firms take advantage of the new low-wage sector in the area, notably immigrants and women, where labour organisation is weak and undeveloped. The valiant but ultimately unsuccessful attempt to unionise the large (140-150 workers) Spiralynx factory at Canning Town in the late 1970s illustrates just how difficult it is to organise immigrant workers who do not speak each others' languages, let alone that of the trade union officials. About 50 per cent of the Spiralynx workforce was Tamil or Malayalee South Indians, many of whom had worked in the British Naval Dockyard in Singapore before it closed in 1970 and were recent immigrants to Britain. Other workers included Punjabi, Gujerati, Pakistani and West Indian workers as well as a handful of white British workers.

The Spiralynx management was particularly intransigent and anti-union and appears to have had a policy of isolating ethnic groups; several workers were placed in sections of the factory where only one other person spoke the same language. At the slightest hint of union activity workers were sacked, although it was often difficult to prove in an industrial tribunal that this was because of their audacity to join a trade union. The difficulties of organising workers fearful for their long term residence in this country, their safety from racial attacks and worried about job security, cannot be over-emphasised. In smaller firms, the difficulties only increase. The task of organising a workforce fragmented into small workshops and divided by gender and ethnic groupings remains as difficult today as it did a century ago — perhaps even more so today than in the 1880s because there is a general feeling of demoralisation which is rooted in the overall decline of the furniture making trade in East London.

95

Furniture maker: East End 1986
(David Dilley)

Chapter Four

TALKING ABOUT THE TRADE:
A Selection of Reminiscences About the East London Furniture Trade 1850-1987

Henry Mayhew
Extract from a letter to the Morning Chronicle, 22nd
August 1850

Women's Industrial News, March 1902

Arthur Harding: extract from 'East End Underworld:
Chapters in the Life of Arthur Harding' by Raphael
Samuel, 1983

Alfred Alexander, cabinet maker, b1908

George Wood, cabinet maker and turner, b1903

Sissy Lewis, sprayer, b1914

Jock Shanley, upholster and trade union official, b1902

Henry Doncaster, polisher b1936

Nathan Rosenberg, cabinet maker, b1908

TALKING ABOUT THE TRADE: A Selection of Reminiscences About the East London Furniture Trade 1850-1987

There are several reasons why it is important that furniture workers such as those in this section should tell us about their jobs and daily life. Firstly it helps break the silence that surrounds so much of working life both in the past and today. Secondly it increases the value and respect we all should have for the products of other people's labour. And lastly it gives an insight into the complex nature of the work process itself.

Each day we use the products of the furniture maker's skill; yet it is likely that the circumstances that surrounded, and were central to, the making of the chair, table or whatever are unknown to us. Most of all we are likely to think of furniture as the product of one hand, when in reality it has almost always been the work of many acting together in concert.

The number of different skills that go to make up a piece of furniture are many and change over time; so what appears below can only hint at some of them. In no way does the selection set out to give details of a whole trade or a representative sample of all involved. Such a task would require a seperate book for each.

The selection begins with the words of three cabinet makers taken from one of nine letters on London's woodworking trades published by the pioneering social investigator Henry Mayhew in the *Morning Chronicle* in August and September 1850.

Women's role in the furniture industry in East London has largely been restricted to the finishing trades; notably upholstery and polishing. As little has yet been found of women talking directly about their work in the nineteenth or early twentieth century when many thousands were employed in these trades, we have used an indirect report about women polishers taken from the *Women's Industrial News* of March 1902.

The next seven extracts are all taken from sound recorded interviews with former and present furniture makers. What we have printed is not the full transcript of these interviews but an edited version of parts made by the interviewer with the full permission of the interviewee.

We begin with an extract from Raphael Samuel's book, *East End Underworld: Chapters in the Life of Arthur Harding* , which was originally recorded in the 1970s and published in 1983. All the others were recorded during conversations with Rodney Mace in 1986 and 1987. Copies of these tapes and their transcripts are available for study at the Geffrye Museum.

(The ordering of the extracts is roughly chronological covering a period from 1907 to the early 1960s.) All the people included here were or still are directly involved in furniture production as skilled craftmen and women. Three were active in the trade union movement, Alfred Alexander, Sissy Lewis and Jock Shanley. The remaining four, Arthur Harding, George Wood, Henry Doncaster and Nathan Rosenberg were never members and saw no reason to be so. This division fairly reflects the degree of union organisation in the trade during this period. Family ties were an important dimension of the trade, for it was either through working for a parent (usually the father) that people like George Wood, Nathan Rosenberg and Henry Doncaster came into the business or, in the case of Sissy Lewis because her mother was already doing women's work at Lebus's factory and daughters were expected to follow on. For Alfred Alexander his choice of first employment was limited to those areas open to the immigrant Jewish community at the time. Jock Shanley is an immigrant of a different sort, for it was education in the labour movement that brought him to London from Aberdeen first as an upholsterer and later as a full-time trade union official. Whatever their individual difference they all share the ability to talk in some detail about what they did and how they did it.

One common feature to almost all the extracts is the experience of war production from 1940 to 1945 and the hopes engendered in the post-war period for a more prosperous and for some, a less cut-throat industry. But the reality was to be very different for in the forty years since 1945 the industry has dramatically contracted leaving an almost indelible sadness in people's hearts. This is not the regret for 'the good old days' but a genuine grief for all those skills that are probably lost for ever.

Henry Mayhew
Extract from a letter to the Morning Chronicle, 22nd August 1850

Between October 1849 and December 1850 Henry Mayhew published eighty-two letters in the *Morning Chronicle* detailing the life and work of London's poor. Nine of these were on woodworkers, including a lengthy description on the cabinet making trades that accompanied the direct testimony we reprint below. In 1861 an edited version of all the letters appeared as the now famous volume *London Labour and the London Poor*. However for some reason much of the woodworkers' letters were left out and we had to wait until 1970 when Eileen Yeo and E. P. Thompson published their *Unknown Mayhew* for a fuller version to become available.

The Budget of a Garret Master's Family

From a man who, with his wife and young child, occupied rather a decent room in Spitalfields, I had the following statement as to his mode of living. He was a fancy cabinet maker:

'I get up always at six, summer and winter. I wake natural at that hour, if I'm ever so tired when I go to bed and sleep ever so dead. If it's summer I go to work in the daylight at six; if it's winter by candle-light. My wife gets up an hour after me. Indeed she can't well sleep in the room I'm working in. (We've only one room.) She makes the fire and boils the kettle, and gets breakfast ready at eight. It's coffee and bread and butter. I may take ten minutes to it, sometimes only five. She has dinner ready at one, and that's coffee and bread and butter three days at least in the week, and that's finished in ten minutes too. Then I've tea, not coffee, for a change about five, and I go to bed at ten without any supper — except on Sundays — after sixteen hours' labour, just with a few breaks, as I've told you. Most people in my way, who are badly off as I am, work on Sundays. All that I know do, but *I* don't. I haven't strength for it after sixteen hours' work a day for six days, so I rest on Sunday, and stay in bed till twelve or after. When we haven't coffee for dinner we have a bit of cheap fish — mackerel at $1\frac{1}{2}$d or 1d a piece, or soles at 2d a pair, and a potato with it. Sometimes they're almost as cheap as coffee for dinner. For breakfast for me, my wife, and a child five years old, coffee, half an ounce, costs $\frac{1}{2}$d; bread and butter $3\frac{1}{2}$d — 1d butter, and 2d bread. Dinner the same, but an ounce of coffee instead of half an ounce as at breakfast; so that's $4\frac{1}{2}$d, and about the same if it's fish, or 1d or $1\frac{1}{2}$d more, but there isn't as much fish as we could eat. Tea's $\frac{1}{2}$d more than breakfast. No supper, and to bed at ten. On Sundays we have mostly half a bullock's head, which costs 10d to 1s. We have it boiled, with an onion and a potato to it; or when we're hard up we have it without either for dinner, and warm it for supper. There's none left for Monday sometimes, and never much. I don't taste beer above once a month, if that. In winter, fire and candlelight cost me 3s to 4s a week for some weeks, or 4s 6d a week when there's fog, for my place isn't very light, and I'm forced to burn candles all day long then, and I must have a bit of fire all times for my glue-pot. There have been times — but things are cheaper now, though work's not so brisk — when we've had no butter to our bread, and hardly a crumb of sugar to our coffee. My rent is 1s 10d a week, and my own sticks. It costs at least 7s to keep us, and that's 8s 10d altogether. I don't earn more than 12s a week the year through, so that the extra fire and candle in the winter takes it every farthing, and more; and then we're forced to go without butter. There's 3s 2d, say, left in summer time for clothing, and all that; but I haven't bought a new thing that way since I got married seven years back. My wife earns, perhaps, 2s a week at charing, but her health's bad. I work for a slaughterer; not one in particular, but one is my principal customer. I began as a little master when I'd been a fortnight out of my time. My mother lent me 20s. She's middling off, and in service. I'd picked up tools before. Then my wife had saved on to £5 in service, which furnished the room, with what I made myself. I think most of us marry servants that have saved a trifle. A good many have, I know. My little girl's too young to do anything now, but she must work at lining with her mother when she's old enough. Children soon grow to be useful, that's one good thing. She goes to a Sunday school at present, and is learning to read.'

But the usual assistants of the small masters are their own children. Upon this subject I received the following extraordinary statement:

'The most on us has got large families. We put the children to work as soon as we can. My little girl began about six, but about eight or nine is the usual age.' 'Ah, poor little things,' said the wife, 'they're obliged to begin the very minute they can use their fingers at all. The most of the cabinet makers of the East End have from five to six in family, and they are generally all at work for them. The small masters mostly marry when they are turned of twenty. You see our trade's come to such a pass that unless a man has children to help him he can't live at all...'

'Just look at her,' he continued, producing a rosewood tea caddy. It was French polished, lined with tinfoil, and with lock and key. 'Now, what do you think we got for that, materials, labour, and all? Why, 16d; and out of that there's only 4d for the labour. My wife and daughter polishes and lines them, and I make them, and all we get is 4d, and we have to walk perhaps miles to sell them for that.'

'Why I stood at this bench,' said the wife, 'with my child, only ten years old, from four o'clock on Friday morning till ten minutes past seven in the evening, without a bit to eat or drink. I never sat down a minute from the time I began till I finished my work, and then I went out to sell what I had done. I walked all the way from here (Shoreditch) down to the Lowther Arcade, to get rid of the articles.' Here she burst in a violent flood of tears, saying, 'Oh, sir, it is hard to be obliged to labour from morning till night as we do — all of us, little ones and all — and yet not to be able to live by it either.' 'Why, there's Mr ——, the warehouseman, in——,' the husband went on, 'offered me £6 a gross for the making of these very caddies, as I showed just now, and that would have left me only $\frac{1}{2}$d a dozen for my labour. Why, such men won't let poor people remain honest.'

'And you see, the worst of it is this here — children's labour is of such value now in our trade that there's more brought into the business every year, so that it's really for all the world like breeding slaves. Without my children I don't know how we should be able to get along. There's that little thing,' said the man, pointing to the girl of ten years before alluded to, as she sat at the edge of the bed, 'Why, she works regularly every day from six in the morning till ten at night. She never goes to school; we can't spare her. There's schools enough here for a penny a week, but we could not afford to keep her without working. If I'd ten more children I should be obligated to employ them all the same way... Of the two thousand five hundred small masters in the cabinet line, you may safely say that two thousand of them, at the very least, has from five

to six in a family, and that's upwards of 12,000 children that's been put to the trade since the prices has come down. Twenty years ago I don't think there was a young child at work in our business, and I'm sure there isn't now a small master whose whole family doesn't assist him. But what I want to know is, what's to become of the 12,000 children when they're grow'd up, and come regular into the trade? Here are all my young ones growing up without being taught anything but a business that I know they must starve at.'

had in case of sickness? 'Oh, bless you,' he said, 'there's nothing but the parish for us. I did belong to a benefit society about four years ago, but I couldn't keep up my payments any longer. I was in the society above five-and-twenty years, and then was obliged to leave it after all. I don't know of one as belongs to any friendly society, and I don't think there is a man as can afford it in our trade now. They must all go to the workhouse when they're sick or old.'

An elderly man, with a heavy careworn look, whom I found at work with his wife and family, gave me the following information concerning his occupation as a *little master*. He was then engaged in making tea caddies, his wife and daughter being engaged in 'lining' workboxes for the husband's next employment. They resided in a large room, a few steps underground, in a poor part of Spitalfields. It was very light, from large windows both back and front, and was very clean. A large bed stood in the centre, and what few tables and chairs there were were old and mean, while the highly polished rosewood tea caddies, which were placed on a bare deal table, showed in startling contrast with all the worn furniture around. The wife was well spoken and well looking; and the daughter, who was also well-looking, had that almost painful look of precocity which characterises those whose childhood is one of toil:

'I have been upwards of 40 years a fancy cabinet maker,' the man said, 'making tea caddies and everything in that line. When I first worked on my own account I could earn £3 a week. I worked for the trade then, for men in the toy, or small furniture, or cabinet line only. There was no slaughter shops in those days. And good times continued till about 21 years ago, or not so much. I can't tell exactly, but it was when the slaughter houses came up. Before that, on a Saturday night, I could bring home, after getting my money, a new dress for my wife, for I was just married then, and something new for the children when they came, and a good joint for Sunday. Such a thing as a mechanic's wife doing needlework for any but her own family wasn't heard of then, as far as I know. There was no slop needlewomen in the wives of my trade. It's different now. They must work some way or other. Me and my father before me, for he brought me up to the business, used to supply honourable tradesmen at a fair price, finding our own material; all the family of us is in the trade, but there was good times then. This part didn't then swarm with slaughter houses, as it does now. I think there's fifty at this end of the town. I have to work harder than ever. Sometimes I don't know how to lie down of a night to rest best, from tiredness. The slaughtermen give less and less. My wife and family help me, or I couldn't live. I have only one daughter now at home, and she and my wife line the work boxes as you see. I have to carry my goods now, and have for 15 years or more hawked to the slaughter houses. I carried them out on a sort of certainty, or to order, before that. I carry them out complete, or I needn't carry them out at all.'

'I've now been on tea caddies, 12 inch, with raised tops. The materials — rosewood veneers, deal, locks, hinges, glue and polish — cost me £1 for a dozen. I must work hard and very long hours, 13 or more a day, to make two dozen a week, and for them I only get at the warehouse 28s a dozen if I can sell them there. That's 16s a week for labour. Sometimes I'm forced to take 25s — that's 10s a week for labour. Sometimes I bring them back unsold. Work boxes is no better pay, though my wife and daughter line them. If I get an order — and that's very seldom, not once a year — for a number of tea caddies, I must take them in at a certain time, because they're mostly for shipping, and so I must have some help. But I can't get a journeyman to help me unless I can show him he'll make 15s a week, because he knows I just want him for a turn, and can't do without him, and so the profit goes off. Old men can't work quick enough. They may be employed when there's no particular hurry. If I'm not to time with a shipping order, it's thrown on my hands.... No man on my earnings, which is 15s some weeks, and 10s others, and less sometimes, can bring up a family as a family ought to be brought up. Many a time I've had to pawn goods that I couldn't sell on a Saturday night to rise a Sunday's dinner.' 'Yes, indeed,' interposed the wife, 'look you here, sir; here's forty or fifty duplicates (producing them) of goods in pawn. If ever we shall get them out, Lord above knows...'

Portrait of Henry Mayhew
From a daguerreotype by Beard, published in **London Labour and the London Poor** *1861-2*
(Photo Studios)

Women's Industrial News, March 1902

The Women's Industrial News *was published regularly between 1895 and 1919 as the Journal of the Women's Industrial Council that campaigned vigorously for women to enter industry in the 'spirit of a fair field and no favour'. In this case it was for women to extend their polishing skills into those areas that were still seen as men's work.*

> ...the polishing trade in London belongs to Hoxton, Shoreditch, Bethnal Green and Hackney, and a little to the EC district.

Among the cabinet makers, furniture dealers, upholsterers, french polishers, lurks the polisher who employs women; it is possible that he does polishing if he calls himself any one of these titles, and equally possible that he may do no polishing, though 'Polisher' is writ large over his shop.

> Investigator searching, when she has plunged valiantly into the shop, or as is more often the case, climbed the steep narrow unwashed sort of ladder staircase at the top of which French polishers love to live, it is probably only to be told, 'No, I don't employ women, but so and so round the corner does.' So round the corner she — it was always a she investigator in this case — goes with renewed hopes; only to be sent round a fresh corner again to fresh disappointments.

As an actual fact there are few large employers of women, they are chiefly employed by the small man who works for some retail shop or for the trade, and employs from 16 to 20 men and women, the men polishing the large furniture, the women the small, both working in the same workrooms. More common than that is the employer (and frequently the employer is a woman) who in his own house in a slum off the main streets of Shoreditch and Hoxton, puts up 'French Polisher' over his door, and in his own front parlour, employs two, three or four girls. These 'hole in the corner' workshops account for the difficulty in finding employers of women. Lastly, much polishing is done in the homes, and this of course means women's labour.

> The conclusion one arrives at as a result of investigation is that the manufacture of inferior goods, generally speaking, implies the employment of ill-paid and improperly trained labour. Certainly this is the case in

French polishing. The women, who polish inferior made goods, do not need the training and do not earn as much as those who polish inlaid work.

A good piece of furniture passes through several processes before it is ready to take the polish. It is sand-papered and then stained. Then the process known as 'bodying in' takes place, i.e. the wood is rubbed with a mixture of Plaster of Paris and linseed oil since neither planing nor sand-papering gives sufficiently smooth surface to receive the best polish. This is rubbed in vigorously and fills up every unevenness in the surface. The surplus is wiped off with a rag. Suppose the furniture to be imitation Sheraton before the staining takes place, the process called 'stopping' must be performed. That is to say, the little beading of self-coloured wood must be protected from the stain. This is done by giving a coat of varnish to the required edge before the wood is stained, and is a delicate process. The polishing then begins — the pad, made of cotton wool covered with a piece of rag, dipped in the polishing mixture, and the work at this stage is chiefly a matter of much rubbing and elbow grease. Often a piece of furniture is put away after its first polish, and a day or two after taken out again to go through the process a second time. Finally it is well rubbed with a pad dipped in methylated spirits to take off the excess of oil.

> As will be seen, the work is purely manual, requiring very little intelligence. In the cheaper branches of the work — the polishing of cheap chests and over mantels — very little skill and nicety is required. It is merely a matter of staining the requisite shade and rubbing until the surface acquires a certain amount of 'shine'. In the better class of work it is often claimed to be an art; and it is said that a great deal of training and intelligence is required to understand how to get the right shade of stain and the right surface before beginning to polish; that different sorts of wood require different treatment, and this can only be aquired by experience and the exercise of intelligent observation. This accounts for the different requirements in different workshops. A firm where cheap furniture receives a dash of stain and a certain amount of polishing needs a different style of worker from the the polishing of

imitation Sheraton; and the length of time spent learning the trade varies accordingly. Any time between six months to three years seems to be the length of training, and it is obvious that in a workshop professing to polish only a few light articles of furniture a girl has learnt her trade, as far as that shop is concerned, in a short time; whereas a girl in a firm which undertakes to polish all kinds of furniture in all sorts of styles will, as the foremen are fond of saying, 'have never finished learning.'

Girls begin to learn the trade at about 14 or 15 years of age. They are paid a weekly wage of 2s 6d, 3s 6d or 4s for the first six months; and this is raised as the girl improves in her work; but she is usually considered a learner or improver for two or three years and earns during the last part of that time 7s, 8s or 10s. Many firms do not take learners, but there appears to be no difficulty in getting competent hands from those who do. In such firms the forewoman teaches, but old hands will tell you they 'learnt it off their father.'

The trade is in a curious transition state, and seems to be passing into the hands of women, and it is interesting to compare certain results of this investigation with a somewhat smaller one carried out some two years ago. Then the investigator came to the conclusion that the trade was a suitable one for girls in its lighter branches — i.e. the polishing of smaller things — cricket bats, overmantels, looking glass frames and the like — but the heavy work was done by men and fit only for men. Further, that the number of women employed in the trade was increasing, and that the demand for them was great. Today, however, girls are employed in polishing large furniture, seemingly with no bad results to themselves or to the work. Often large pieces of furniture are taken to pieces and the women then polish the pieces, or men are called in to move heavy furniture into the required position. Then it seems not harder work to rub a large surface than a small one. As regards the number of women employed, we are told now that there is not work enough for those already in the trade. A number are out of work — the trade is slack — 'because of the War.' Of course there are those who, employing only men, assert that this is a trade unfit for women, that it is too hard, too dirty, too demoralising; there are the more enlightened who say it is a trade which in its lighter branches, is quite suited to women, and a desirable trade could certain disadvantages such as sharing the same workrooms with men be obviated; there are the practical who say nothing, but employ women in all the branches of the trade with great success. The obvious reason for this employment is the same all trades through — they are cheaper — a woman time worker receives from 3d to 5d an hour as compared with a man's 9d; they are less trouble, which, being interpreted, means they do not strike, they do not drink, they are more amenable to authority, they are more regular in their hours — a French polisher is frequently most erratic in the number of hours or days per week he will work.

And lastly, almost invariably, it was stated that women were more conscientious and thorough in their work. In one house, where, by dint of much perseverance, we had discovered in a top room three women polishers at work, we were told by the eldest of them that men polishers were employed as well as women, but the women did the 'fiddling' work — i.e. the carved backs of chairs. 'Do you suppose a man would bother to polish in them cracks and holes?' was the contemptuous query. 'He wouldn't take the trouble'. As a matter of fact, he cannot afford to spend the time, as though he may be a time worker, he is expected to produce a certain amount in a certain number of hours. In a firm employing both men and women, the foreman told us that the women did precisely the same work as the men, except in the few cases where the furniture was heavy and could not be taken to pieces, and received one half or a third of the wages paid the men. 'Why?' we asked, for this was a non-Union firm. 'Ah! that is a question you must solve; I'm often puzzled about it.' 'Is there any difference in the quality of work?' 'No, I prefer women's work — they are more conscientious and take a pride in their work; they often get a fine finish and have a greater perception of detail and more delicacy of work.' 'Do they work less quickly?' 'A little, but not appreciably and that is quite compensated for by the excellence of their work.'

'Are the restrictions against overtime a hindrance to them?' 'Not at all, though the men work overtime in the very occasional rushes that occur, this is not sufficient to account for the low wages paid to women.'

Afterwards, as we walked through the workshop, the forewoman showed us with great pride a suite of furniture executed for the 'governor', and told with great pride how she and an apprentice had polished the whole of the suite, and how difficult certain parts of it had been, and what an honour it was considered by the apprentice to be chosen to help her.

As far as the desirability of the trade for women is concerned, one can say little. If women are to enter industry seriously, in the spirit of a fair field and no favour, they must take the rough with the smooth; and there is no doubt that good opening though polishing may be for a certain class of girls, it is one which at present attracts only a very rough, low class. This view one naturally is inclined to combat at first: but it is the first statement that an employer or a foreman will make, 'If you are trying to find a nice trade for a girl, don't put her to the polishing; there is not denying that though it is a skilled trade, and a well paid trade, we only get the rough class of girls in here. A polisher came to me the other day, and said, 'I should like to put my girl to the trade, because it's a good one, but I don't think I could stand the people she would have to mix with.' One young foreman was very bitter and said, 'If you get two or three good girls, they mix with the others, and get as bad as them in a week, they haven't a chance. They are put to work with the men — and polishers are proverbially a bad lot — and they hear all the bad language and worse that goes on. There are no arrangements for girls of any kind, so how can they keep decent?' The woman, whom we found working with two others on the top floor, was of the same opinion. She had been in the trade for 20 years. 'I would never put a girl of mine to the trade', she said. 'It is all right up here, we don't mix with the men, but as soon as we leave here, we may have to. Most of the girls have to, and you get a nice girl in, and in a month she's like the rest of them.' Moreover, polishing is a dirty trade. It is only the rough class of girl who will consent habitually to be dirty, with hands almost always stained. The splashes of stain and handling of oil tend to make polishers even less attractive in appearance than the majority of factory hands. These two factors, in conjunction with the insanitary premises, tend to keep polishing in the hands of the very rough and very poor. As regards wages, polishing since it is a skilled trade compares favourably with other trades — 14s, 15s, up to 20s a week are the usual earnings.

As regards conditions generally, they are good. Hours are often somewhat shorter than are allowed by law. Overtime is practically unknown. It cannot be called a season trade, though there is a busy time. The work is not unhealthy. Some say that the methylated spirit is wholesome — certainly it is not unpleasant — and the smell of stain is not sufficiently pungent to be injurious. It is true that a girl has to stand to do her work and that the rubbing is hard, but the muscles soon grow accustomed to the continual movement. A few cannot use a certain stain, it produces sores and a sort of skin disease, but this is peculiar to very few. Nevertheless, the premises on which polishing is carried on are often not the most salubrious. Where there is a fairly large firm the accomodation is good, but where polishing is carried on by a small employer, the girls work in a wretched house in a slum. There is none of the loftiness and light and spaciousness, which a

factory built as such, to accomodate a good many hands, possesses. There may be the requisite number of cubic feet per head for each worker, and the allotted portion of light, but a very little experience of this kind convinces the investigator that factory legislation deals gently with employers and in this respect at least the advantages of a large factory system over a small one, and factory work over home work are very clearly borne in upon her. There is, moreover, no law which says 'You shall scrub your stairs and floors, and sometimes wash the few windows you possess', and consequently the work done under small employers is done in about as insanitary conditions as it is possible to imagine.

One further undesirable feature in the trade is the amount of home work done. To any one who has seen a little of home work, such a trade is always a doubtful one to recommend a girl to enter. Even if, while unmarried, she earns good wages under good conditions at a factory, the fact that she may drift after marriage into the position of an outworker, with all its attendant miseries, is an enormous disadvantge. To wait about for work where men of an avowedly rough type are employed; to take home work needing much room, in an already not too roomy establishment: work, moreover, which encourages dirty rather than clean surroundings, which means that the family lives in an atmosphere of spirit and stain, that children may be called on to take a share in work which, at any rate, is too hard for them; that it should be possible, as we were told, for a girl to work all day at a factory and then go home to a father who was a polisher at home and work for him till 12 or 1 o'clock at night — these are grave disadvantages to any trade.

Nevertheless, despite these disadvantages, hopeful signs are not lacking. Home work is never a satisfactory form of work to employers, and is said to be dying out. Whether it will altogether is doubtful, and it is of course convenient both to employer and employee, and as an occasional method cannot be objected to. The great objection, in our opinion, is that there should be a class of workers who are by profession outworkers, and who are the worst paid, the most overworked, and who, working themselves under the worst conditions, draw other labour which is unpaid into their own miserable lot.

Further, though at present women work chiefly for small firms under bad conditions, or for larger firms in the same workrooms with men, there are a few firms larger still which show the possibility of better things. The conditions in one large factory may serve as an illustration. Men and women are both employed, but the women work in a separate room, and have separate accomodation, they leave the factory at different hours and never meet the men. The room in which we saw the women working was large and light and lofty; it was in this factory that it was said the women did as good work as the men, they served a three years' apprenticeship and earned 14s to 20s a week. There was no overtime and none desired. Nevertheless, the foreman volunteered the information that the trade still only attracted the low class of girl before alluded to, and suggested that it was because of the tradition attaching to the trade, and was a case of 'give a dog a bad name.' While admitting that by improving conditions, the girls might grow gentler too, he was of the opinion that the stained hands and the nature of the work would always attract to the trade only the rough-est of factory hands. And indeed it does not seem probable that the work of polishing will pass into the hands of large employers, for it is work requiring small plant and small premises.

The trade will probably remain largely in the hands of the small employer, i.e. the man who employs 14 or 15 men and women, and the 'polisher' with whom it is more or less a family affair — his employees being wife and daughters, with possibly a neighbour or two thrown in. Such employers are naturally unenlightened, and necessarily, from force of circumstances, far from ideal.

Desirable or not, there is no doubt that women are, and will be, increasingly employed, both by reason of cheapness, and the excellence of their work...

Arthur Harding: extract from 'East End Underworld: Chapters in the Life of Arthur Harding' by Raphael Samuel, 1983

Arthur Harding was born in Bethnal Green in 1886. Besides being a cabinet maker, Arthur Harding was a street trader and a wardrobe dealer. He was at various times of his life involved in crime, and four years after the events related below, served a five year prison sentence for his part in the 'Vendetta Affair', and later did a five year spell at Dartmoor.

In 1907 — when I was nineteen or twenty — I started a cabinet-maker's factory in partnership with a man named Bill Saville who had had a long experience of the work. Bill lived in Chilton Street. He worked in a cellar there and made cheap china cabinets. He owed my sister £20. I was only there to get our money back. I put a few quid in, but I could see I wasn't going to get rich so I turned it in.

The first place we had was at the back of a pub in Hare Street — called Cheshire Street now — the 'Red Cross'. We took the back part for a workshop, me and Bill Saville and a workman we employed. We took it 'cause the rent was very cheap, 5s a week, something like that. The room was supposed to be a bagatelle room. It belonged to the pub. You had to carry the timber up the side of the pub, through a passageway. We did very well there but they sold the pub. It was one of the pubs done away with by a Liberal Act of Parliament which got rid of thousands of pubs. After we left, it was turned into the synagogue, 'cause the number of Jewish people was increasing enormously around there.

Then we got a place in Cotton's Gardens. It was in a turning off Kingsland Road, opposite Drysdale Street. It was a factory which had just been built. We had the bottom floor. Upstairs was all in the boot trade. It was a big place — we could have got a dozen makers and their benches in there and it was much more expensive than Hare Street — 15s a week. We only took it because they didn't know us. We had to knock them in the end for five week's rent. We never paid anybody for anything. Saville was well known for that — that's why he put my name on the bill. We bought the timber from the place opposite and never paid them. 'Long firm' business. We were able to do it because we looked a posh affair.

Our speciality was making Louis cabinets. They were flash jobs with big mirrors on the sides, and ornaments. Cameo legs, glass all bevelled. They stood at least 7 foot high with the pediment at the top. There was a big pane of glass in the middle, and two kidney-shaped mirrors at the sides, fitted into the wood, and a diamond shape at the bottom. There were two doors underneath with shelves to put in crockery and glasses, all that sort of thing. The whole thing was a gigantic bluff. They were very cheap to make for they looked expensive. I suppose they sold them for about a tenner each. Louis cabinets were made out of whitewood blacked all over; the polishers stained them black and then used to polish them with a varnish, not french polishing but sandpaper and varnish. A wee bit of carving, and that was it.

We had four makers and a couple of polishers. They didn't have no planing to do — the work was all planed and cut at the mill. All they had to do was fit them up. I wasn't much of a cabinet maker — I'm a carpenter — but there was no hard work in it. Whitewood — they don't use it today — would take the stain and polish easy. The drawer had a bit of carving on the front of it — what they called 'a scratching'. There wasn't any artistic fittings, they was nailed and glued together. The carving cost 5s 6d. I used to get my brother's father-in-law, Mr. Gibbs to do the carving. He was a good carver.

The cabinet would cost some 25s for making, that is 5s for maker, 5s for timber, 5s for polisher and polish, 5s for glass, 5s for carving. Nails was 2d a pound. When completed they were sold to the large wholesalers in the Curtain Road. Each maker would make six cabinets a week. Really and truly they cost us about 27s or 28s to make, and we used to sell them to Hollington's for 32s. I don't think we ever got more than 32s out of them. Hollington's was the last resort. They kept open till 5 o'clock on the Saturday afternoon. The workmen used to wait for us to come back after selling them, so that they could get their wages: they waited just by the railway arch in Kingsland Road, in a pub.

If the work was ordered by a shop you might get 40s or more. But if you had no orders you had to take them out on spec. It was a bare living. No matter how many of them you made, you wouldn't get rich.

Jack Taylor, he'd come round with his pony and cart and he'd say, 'Got anything? — I'm going round Dulwich or Hammersmith', or something like that. He worked the furniture shops round there. It was a question of transport — he had a pony and cart. He used to go round hawking. Lewisham was a good place. The shopkeepers there would say, 'Well let me have a couple of them. I'll try them,' and he'd probably sell them for 5Os a piece. There was an art in selling them to the shops.

Saville did the work, I owned the shop. I helped him to mark the wood out, but the workmen did most of the work. We engaged some six makers and two polishers. Monday no workmen appeared, it seems that Monday was devoted to drinking beer. The day was regarded as a holiday which started by having a sub from the boss — this was the custom in the cabinet making business. While the men spent their money on drink, we the bosses would buy the timber for the week's work and during the morning we would visit the wholesalers for orders. Tuesday the makers would start work, marking out the wood for the mill to cut and plane. The day's work would end about 7 to 8 pm. Most workers would ask for a sub to carry on at home. The rest of the week they would work hard.

It didn't last long — not more than about a couple of months. If we'd had our own horse and vans we could have made a profit. Saville was a man that knew the business right through, but he was too fond of women and you can't mix it — when I was earning money if I'd been out boozing and betting horses I'd never've saved up enough to get meself out of the bloody mess I was in. I set about him and belted him. He went up the nick and got a summons against me and I was given a £10 fine.

Cabinet makers were very numerous in the East End of London. During the years 1890 and onwards, land developers could be seen in every road where there were houses which had gardens in the rear. The gardens were bought from the landlord and the builders would put up small workshops which were let to cabinet makers. Blyth Street and Teesdale Street in Bethnal Green were specially built for the Jewish cabinet makers. The top storey was made for workshops. They were built by a firm named Davis. The houses in Bacon Street was the same. Each tenement had a workshop in the back-yard which had been built on the garden. There was no entrance or exit for the workmen and their work had to be carried through the passage-way of the houses. So one can guess at the filthy conditions of the premises. Nearly in every street there was chairmakers. They didn't finish the chair, only frames. They sold them in the white to the uphol-

sterers. Mostly birch. You would have a couple of benches. You could stack them on top of each other. There was not much work in it, planing them. The mill done all the work. The upholsterers finished them, polished them, got them ready for market. There were plenty of buyers — people were changing from Windsor chairs to upholstered chairs. Light's in Curtain Road were the big buyers. They bought for the West End. Chair making was a trade by itself. You didn't move from it to cabinet making. They kept to that one branch of the business.

Then there were the barrow-makers or wheelwrights. They made barrows and let them out at one shilling a day. I know one man — Goldfine — who made a fortune out of it. Everybody wanted market barrows.

Cabinet making was a family affair. You brought up your chidren to it. Then Darling & Son set up in 1902. They was printers. They brought printing to the East End. They took all the boys from St. Matthew's. Instead of going into the cabinet-making they went into the print and turned out more respectable. Some of the biggest ruffians out had children who did that. It was a very respectable firm, with commissionaires on the door.

Overmantels was the easiest thing for a man to make. Everybody bought overmantels. It was a new fashion about 1900. The poor always wanted an overmantel. Couldn't have a house without an overmantel. We had one in Queen's Buildings. The bigger the better. Lovely glass in the middle and two side glasses. They was all different types. Some had shelves on, most did, and a canopy at the top, with a big shelf to put little ornaments on, or a clock. The one we had at Queen's Buildings was just a cheap thing, about ten bob I suppose. It looked all right. Polished, not painted. You had two little fasteners on both sides, you put the nail through into the wall, and that was it. They was very ornate, black and gold. Ours was polished walnut. Overmantels wasn't expensive. The cheapest were ten bob new in a shop. When you looked at 'em, you couldn't realise how cheap they was.

I knew a lot of overmantel makers, cabinet makers you know, who made them. They'd take them on the hawk, round the retail shops, save a shop at Croydon making the long journey to the East End. My father used to make them, to have 'em gilded and all — he had a craftsman gilder to do it. I made overmantels too. You could make half a dozen at a time. The whole thing was really cheap — a couple of panels, several panes of looking-glass and plenty of stain. You could use any kind of wood and buy a cheap stain. Fox's in

Church Street, the chemists, they sold polishes and stains.

Cabinets — like china cabinets or music cabinets — were the same. Polished wood, everything that was made was polished. Veneered, no — you see years ago they had this system of inlaying. They used small instruments and they put a screw through the piece of wood, half inch or one inch according to how far they wanted the marking to go and then they put a sort of yellow line in it. Well, that's how they made inlaid furniture. The end of the screw cut into the soft wood, and left a ridge. Then all they had to do was put the inlaid stuff in, and you had an inlaid top, which made it look a very precious thing. It didn't cost nothing. Sold 'em for 8s.

About 1900 the Hackney Furnishing Company started the shilling business — you know, the credit business. You could buy a five pound home for a shilling a week. 'Five pounds — a hundred weeks to pay,' that's what their adverts said. It stands out in my memory. It was such a huge success that other firms copied. You got a kitchen table, a couple of chairs, a Windsor chair, a bed, and a wash hand-stand. From the business point of view it was a wonderful idea because after a couple had been in it a year or two, they would find something else that they wanted. It might be a wardrobe, or a china cabinet. It was such a wonderful idea because you had to go there, most cases on a Saturday when you had your money in your pocket. If they were decent people they would aspire for a better home than what they had. So, the result was that when they went there they'd probably buy something extra.

The wash hand-stand was really only a wooden top with a round ring in it for the basin and a stand for the jug of water, and then the chamber pot underneath. But some of them was really ornate. They had a composition, like a kind of marble, imitation marble for the top, so that the water when you washed yourself wouldn't sink into the wood and perish it. Composition, it was only composition you know. Not all of 'em, some of 'em just had an ordinary wooden top, cheap like the kitchen table. But they had a little bit of wood at the back so that the bowl wouldn't slip off, or the jug wouldn't slip off. Just a small backing. Some became more ornate; they had a mirror fixed in the middle and side wings and they developed into the three-piece furniture: the sideboard and the wardrobe and the dressing table. In the end you had the dressing table with a lovely mirror in the middle. A bedroom suite was the first furniture I bought when I got married in 1924, to keep the clothes clean of bugs.

The first thing for a couple who could afford it was a wardrobe. Wardrobes were practically unknown when I was a child. You put the same things on the next day. It was a question of sticking them on the chair when you went to bed of a night. If you had any best clothes, you kept them in the pawnshop.

Cabinet making was a precarious living because of the cut-throat competition of the vast number of out-of-work makers who could be seen in the Curtain Road area every day. If you didn't have the orders you still had to keep your men employed or they would go to work for somebody else, and at the end of the week you'd got to sell them because you depended on that to pay your men out. You'd got no capital or bank account. You'd got to sell on Saturday even if you lost money on what you had made. Rivington Street, Shoreditch, had a number of wholesale firms who bought the finished work. They bought black Louis cabinets which cost some 30s to make. Sometimes the maker would be compelled to sell at a loss. Overmantels would be sold sometimes at 10s each. Many small makers were compelled to pay a hawker to travel with a load of work around London's furniture retail shops to sell at a price which did not leave much profit for his labour. Hollington's were a big firm in Rivington Street. It was run by two brothers. They used to buy it pounds cheaper than what it was worth because they knew the cabinet makers had to sell their work on Saturday or Friday in order to have the money to pay the workmen. Lebus, they were one of the worst slave-masters out. I remember pulling the barrow up to their factory in Worship Street. They had their own factory but they bought everything.

Bedroom suites were small then, you could get three or four on a barrow — very small wardrobes, wooden bedstead, wooden coal scuttles with a tin inside them. Nearly every cabinet maker made those. There was plenty of fellows about who'd do a job for 6d, that was nothing unusual. I knew chaps who'd take loads of stuff up to the Cattle Market (that was about eight miles away) for half-a-crown.

Most of these makers depended on buying cheap boards from the timber-yards. There were plenty of timber-yards about. At that time there was no three-ply. You went to the timber merchant and ordered common deal. A 3 inch plank was ripped down to a bare quarter of an inch so they could get 12 out of a plank. They used that for the back-board of a gentleman's wardrobe, or the bottom and panels of a chest of drawers. For a cabinet you'd buy the timber for about 20 or 30 at a time. You bought it to a certain width, according to the shelves you've got in your cabinet, about 4 or 5 inches wide. All you had to do was to fit it up and plane down the raw edges. You had different patterns for the different kinds of cabinets, and you'd follow them.

We sometimes used old packing cases. Firms didn't want to be lumbered with old packing cases. They were glad to get rid of them. The Kemp family in Bacon Street, they used to buy these big barrels, great big barrels which had been used to send over tobacco from America. They used them to make round tables. All the family was at the same business, a big family, a lot of brothers. They had proper workshops all round Bacon Street, Chiltern Street, and they employed people. They were biggish people, but they used to spend their money on beer, so they didn't become millionaires. Dealers would get cases from the city, all they had to do was to take the nails out. Georgie Berner in Bacon Street, he made a living out of it, he knew all the firms which had the stuff — this cheap, whitewood stuff. You could get it yourself, but you had all the trouble of knocking the packing cases to pieces; pulling out the nails, filling up the nail holes. It was easier to buy from a dealer.

In the cabinet making game you were always in debt. You owed the timber-merchant, you owed the glass people. Somebody's got to be done. One week it was the timber-yard, the next it was the glass people, another week the carver, or the people where you went to get the fittings. To survive you had to swindle somebody — you either swindled the timber man or the glass man, or you didn't pay the rent. You'd buy what you could on trust — got it 'on the nod'. One week you'd knock them, the next week you'd pay. The economics of it was not to pay so long as you could get away with it. Say they want to settle on Monday. Well you've no ready money, and so you ask them to wait. You do the same thing with the timber people, the same thing with the glass people, the same with the landlord.

A lot of cabinet makers worked at home. Jimmy Saunders who lived on the Mount was a man who worked for many years in a one-room workshop making wooden brackets for which there was a great demand. Some of his work was very expensive. The brackets were made with a mirror in the middle and shelves held up by pillars. Expensive ones had some good carving. These brackets went in pairs and looked very nice when they had family photographs. Charlie Cooper was an overmantel maker. He had a large room in Turin Street, Bethnal Green. He could make a large stock of overmantels for sale to retail shops. The making was easy but the only snag was getting the bevelled glass for the centre piece. Charlie Cooper had a wife who was a good french polisher, so he was able to finish the jobs right out. All they had was a back room in the house in Turin Street with a 6 foot bench. The work was easy. You don't want a lot of help making overmantels, they're quite easy to make. Jimmy Silk, he was a hawker. He had his wife to make the things which he sold at the fairs to children at holiday times, like rattles. Lived in Bacon Street. He made a packet out of her, she was a very hard-working girl. He sold at Hampstead Heath and Deptford Fair.

Joe Barker worked in a single room — on the corner of Club Row, just one room. Not very big, about 9 foot square, 'cos they wasn't big cabinets. They was only small cabinets that they made. The height was only about 2 foot and the width was about 20 inches — you didn't need a lot of timber.

Not all the cabinet makers were poor. The Mitchells became big-class people. They went from making of 'em to the buying of 'em, sending them all over the world. They were in Bethnal Green Road, at the top of Turin Street. They started round the Mount. There was a lot of brothers. They became pretty wealthy. You wouldn't see them boozing in the public bar, you'd always see them with some customers in the saloon bar. The Taylors was a relation to the Mitchells, but he was more in the selling part of it — they employed him for a time. He had a pony and cart. He was a good seller — he could sell anything.

I knew another cabinet maker who did well — Meadows, he went to school with me. They had a small shop in Bacon Street — they used to make tables, good, decent-class work. The whole family was in the cabinet business. Good tables, good workmanship. I've seen wardrobes go out of there. They bought proper wood at the timber place. They were a family that I would call 'well-breeched'. The daughters were very respectable. They didn't work at cabinet making — they was in the print business. One of them married Jack Godwin, who trained the Jewish boxers. The Meadows were English.

The only time I came into contact with Jewish cabinet-makers was when I lived in Bacon Street. They were Russian Jews. And they were *workers* — the only time they knocked off early was on a Friday.

When we moved round Gibralter Gardens there was two cabinet-makers down there: one was Barclay and the other was old Joe Smith. Jack Barclay made music cabinets. He was a pretty good workman, but he drank. Both he and his wife liked a drop of drink, she was a good goer. He died young of TB. He'd always be round to my sister on a Monday morning to borrow a few bob. He bought a cheap wood and inlaid the top and sides with a home-made tool, using white wax, but heating the wax he was able to inlay the work. He could make a dozen music cabinets a week, price £4 16s 0d. This left him some £2 weekly, not hard work. (These same music cabinets, with three shelves, polished and inlaid, are looked upon as antiques today and sold for £4-£5-£6.) Barclay lived in Gibraltar Buildings where he had a single room. He was just a simple man; a decent chap. I liked him, a very quiet man. He dressed very poorly but he always had a bowler hat — that was unusual for the working class — and he always put on a muffler whatever the weather. When he felt fit enough he'd make a couple of cabinets a day. He'd have to go around fetching the wood. He'd go anywhere he could get it. Orange boxes was ideal. They've got two solid tops and thin sides. They formed the basis of the cabinet and then at the timberyard they sold what they called 'twelve cut', a 2 inch or 3 inch plank of wood cut into 12 very minute boards. You could buy them very cheap and they formed the back part of the cabinet. The shelves were made of the thin part of the orange box — the sides. You didn't pay nothing for 'em. His music cabinets cost 8s, had four shelves in it and stood flat on the ground without any legs. It was really a glorified box with shelves put in, but it looked very nice when it was polished. There was usually a walnut stain, 'cos it was the cheapest and it held the best. And then, at the moment it dried, you gave it a coat of varnish and it come out beautiful. Say it cost him 3Os for somebody else to get him the orange boxes, and nails and screws and a little bit of inlaid stuff, and a wee touch of glue. He'd make very likely about twelve a week, took 'em to Hollington's at the weekend. He made a fair living at it, but he gradually faded away — he had about eight children when he passed away and the oldest boy he died of consumption when he was about fourteen.

Old Joe Smith made music stools. He had one room down Gibraltar Gardens; he used a basement that nobody used, not big, nothing was on a big scale. The basement was about 12 foot by 9 foot. For these music stools he used orange boxes, same as Jack Barclay. It was good wood, clean, no knots in 'em. He got a little smoothing plane, took five minutes to plane 'em up. Then stain it well, and give it a coat of good varnish. All he had to buy was the four legs. Joe Smith didn't have no one to help him — he had a wife but he was always away from her. He did it all himself.

A french polisher could earn more than a cabinet maker, even though she was a woman. It was a skilled trade. The cabinet maker did the work in the white, and the polisher would stain it and varnish and sandpaper. It had to be good work — so beautifully polished that you could see your face reflected in it. The polishers had to polish with a varnish. They made their own rubbers, made a hard ball of wadding, and soaked it in polish. It had to be good quality rag so it wouldn't tear. Then they put a linen rubber over it and

squeezed the polish through.

French polishers didn't work regularly, but any place would take them on. They might do two different firms a week. They would only be taken on when the makers had finished their work, usually at the end of the week. A big firm would have a lot of things for them to make up at the end of the week, and they'd want a couple of polishers. On Friday nights they worked what was called a 'ghoster' — that is they worked all night till Saturday morning — 'cos you had to get the work ready to put in the van and up in Shoreditch. They'd want double the pay for that. They earned enough at the end of the week for the whole week. Women were better polishers than men; they had that uncanny touch. My brother's wife was a polisher. Scores of young women went into it. It was hard work, but paying. A lot of them had the work brought to them at home. It was hard work, handling big wardrobes. You had to keep at it, rubbing, it knocked the hands about. Some of the hooligans married french polishers because they knew they would make good money. The husband might do the woodwork and then leave the wife to do the staining. Charlie Cooper, his wife had her own polishing shop in Turin Street. She used to employ girls to work in there. She was steady, earned plenty of money. She had four or six girls working for her all week. People used to fetch the work to her on the barrow. The husband made his own cabinets, but he liked the drink.

Two very well known characters of the early years of the century were named Sam and Mary Holloway. Both were french polishers and very good at their trade. They would work for six months or more and keep off the drink. He would buy himself some nice clothes and his wife Mary would keep herself nice and tidy. Sam Holloway was a little man, some 5 feet high; his wife was double his size and taller, about 5 foot 1O inches or more. They had a big family and were all well known and respected. When Sam and his wife went on the booze then they lit the neighbourhood up. Mary Holloway was completely changed. From a quiet friendly woman she became a real villain. She could stand and fight any man or woman. I once employed Sam and Mary to polish some work, they were good workers, but when Mary was drunk she would try to sort me out and shout my name all over the place. All the children were polishers, all the sons and all the daughters, they was brought up to it. We paid the Holloways 5s 6d for a Louis cabinet to be glossed. Mrs Holloway was scared of me and everyone else was scared of her. She was a villain when she was drunk, but all right when she was sober. She was a hard worker.

Alfred Alexander, cabinet maker, b1908

Alfred Alexander was born in 1908 in Russia. He was a baby when his parents immigrated with him to Britain, to live in Spital Street, East London. It was, as he put it, 'quite by chance' that he joined the trade which he remained in all his working life: cabinet making.

My father was 43 when he died, in 1926. He'd been ill for eight years before that, so he hadn't been the bread winner for a long time. He had what you would call cancer today; he had a tumour on the back of the spine. He had been a boot maker. My mother was left with five children and we all had to be bread winners, you know. I had another brother who was younger than me — he's since died — and two sisters; and we all worked and produced something and kept the family going.

I decided to become a cabinet maker quite by chance. I was sent to become a farrier and they sent me to somewhere in Shoreditch and I couldn't find the place. This job came up with a man who lived in Code Street off Buxton Street. He had a little house that he shared with his family, with one room which he turned into a cabinet maker's work shop. He used to make bureaux, lovely jobs. He scratched a living of some kind, but he couldn't afford to pay me much, to tell you the truth. I think most of these people became their own masters because they wanted to be on their own and they could cope that way. I got a job with him at 7s 6d a week, chopping out drawer fronts. It was just he and I working.

It was solid oak stuff, and I didn't know how to look after tools at that time; I hadn't been taught yet how to sharpen tools or anything. Anyway, he sharpened the chisels up and I chopped the drawer sides out. They were hand dove tailed. I'd never seen any real furniture before. In my home we had hardly anything, so when I came out into this great world, I thought these bureaux were lovely jobs. Where I lived in Spital Street, just off Brick Lane, there were no furniture shops. There was nothing until you got into Whitechapel Road.

After a time I became dissatisfied and felt 7s 6d wasn't enough, because my mother was a widow by that time, you see. I was advised to go to the Jewish Board of Guardians and ask them if they could find me a job.

They were very very good. They found you a job. You could either be an optician, cabinet maker, or a farrier. I chose to be a cabinet maker because I had some little bit experience of it, and I didn't find it altogether objectionable. They gave me a job in Chambord Street, off Bethnal Green. They gave me an envelope to go and take it to this employer.

When I saw him I got a bit frightened. He had red eyes and looked fierce; but he turned out to be a very kindly man. He was a poor man really, but he wanted to be his own master. At that time cabinet making was very good. You could get a job anywhere. You only had to look in a shop window and see a number of jobs. Anyway, I went there and he accepted me. He had a floor pretty high up; the furniture used to be loaded with a rope on a wheel. I had a guardian, Mr Cohen, who used to come round every month to see how I was getting on, if I was making progress, or hadn't been rude. He'd give me a shilling which was quite a lot of money, out of his own pocket. This chap paid me 25s a week, and he seemed satisfied with me, so they signed me up for four years as an apprentice.

I was to receive half a crown rise every six months. He seemed satisfied with me. First of all, I could write English and read English and he couldn't, so I was useful to him. He had a bank account which made me think he was a wealthy man, till I went into his home. He had hardly any furniture there. He had a houseful of kids. He looked fierce, and he spoke in a very gruff voice, but when he saw I had no father he was very kind. Every Jewish holiday he'd buy me something to wear — a pullover or something like that, outside of what he had to pay me.

This was the first time I saw a wardrobe. You'll never believe this. I hadn't seen a wardrobe before. I didn't know what they were. We used to hang out clothes on a nail on the door. He had some foreign people there who were illiterate, but they made marvellous furniture. I always thought that was peculiar: they can't read or write, yet they've got this skill to make 6 foot wardrobes. They came from Russia, Poland, that part of the world.

I wanted to make modern furniture. I got this bug to want to do it, but in the early days you had to do all the

Alfred Alexander 1953
Addressing a dinner to celebrate the 65th birthday of the chairman of the
NUFTO No. 15 branch, Mr M. Jacobs, who worked at Hille's.
(Alfred Alexander)

rough work. All the wood would be rough wood, stored up on these rafters, and when you wanted to make a job up, you had to pull wood down from the rafters and start working on it from the rough. This was a period when there was hardly any machinery. We had no machinery in the workshop. Everything had to be done by hand, and it was very hard. They gave me all the hard work: for instance, if you wanted a two inch strip from a board, you had to cut it with a hand saw all the way up. It used to make my hands ache. I was only a puny little kid, half starved, suffering from malnutrition, with no real strength. At the end of the day I'd be really knocked out.

Anyway, I survived, and eventually I was able to make my own wardrobe, and a dressing table. This was a period when the suburbs were developing. People were moving out. There was a firm called Drages, who had a big shop in Holborn. Now, Drages were the first to start selling you furniture in a plain van, a shilling a week. It always had to be in a plain van so nobody knew where you came from. In those days it was regarded as a bit of a crime to take things on credit. People felt they didn't like everybody to know that they were getting a home at a shilling a week or so. So naturally the trade became busy. Many a time we'd hire a van for half a crown an hour and take our furniture down to somewhere in the country — or what we called the country — and we'd deposit it there. I used to take some of the furniture down to Drages on a barrow, which we used to hire for 6d an hour. I'd get in the front of the barrow between the shafts, like a horse, a rope round my middle, and pull it all the way from Shoreditch Church, straight down Old Street, to Holborn.

I spent four years there, and after four years he wanted to keep me, and pay me a shilling an hour. I knew by then that the men who were making the furniture there were getting 1s 6d an hour. It doesn't seem much today, but in those days it gave you about £4 a week or so. I didn't want to stay because I thought I was being underpaid. So I left there and went out into the great big wide world, looking for a job.

I found one in one of these shop windows. I didn't know what the world was like outside of the place I worked. The first job I went to did different kind of work, Jacobean work. The first job I got after that was the job with bandings, inlaid work. You'd get a wardrobe panel with mahogany, or curled mahogany, with a thick line of a lighter material. You'd have to fit it in all the way down. You'd get long strips of the material. To scratch it in you would get a piece of wood with a nail in. You cut the end of the nail off and make it sharp. Then you'd scratch, and make an indentation,

so you could get the bandings in. It was like a piece of veneer. Most of the panels were veneered. The first time I tried to do it I made a mess of it. I lasted about two hours there, after which he said, 'I can't afford to keep you'. I'd spoilt the panel.

I wasn't going back to my mother without a job. I got another job at another place, with different kind of work, what they called Sheraton in those days. That was mahogany. The construction was very much the same, but I wasn't fast enough. Where I'd been an apprentice, time didn't matter so much, because I wasn't being paid much. When it came to earning a living for the man and for yourself, it wasn't good enough.

Eventually I found one where I stayed for a while in Hoxton. There again, I was amazed. I'd never seen cocktail cabinets; I'd never made one, I'd never seen one. There was a bloke there who looked anaemic, ill, who couldn't talk English properly, but he could make marvellous cocktail cabinets, with all the bandings in there: beautiful shaped jobs. They hadn't been in this country long enough to learn the language or anything, certainly not to read books on it; they couldn't do that, but they had a great skill. And they didn't work from drawings.

I could tell you a story about that. A Jewish man would find it difficult to get a job in a Gentile firm. (As a matter of fact, I spent all my life trying to get a job in a Gentile firm, and the only time I could get one was during the war, under the Essential Works Order, when they had to accept me.) The story is of one I knew who went to get a job with Maples, in Tottenham Court Road. At that time they had their own factory. I don't think they have now. They made high class furniture. He was a very good cabinet maker, but he couldn't read or write English. This man had been used to being given a photograph of a job — a sideboard, a table, a wardrobe — and he'd make it from that photograph. In those days if you made a job up, you got a photographer who'd come and make a photograph of that, and then you'd try and sell that: a proper photograph. Well, he got to this place, and suddenly they came out with a trolley and all the parts of the job on it, and a drawing. He'd never read a blueprint in his life; he'd never seen one. He looked at this drawing for some time. The foreman came over, and said, 'What's the matter, mate? Any trouble?' 'What's this?' the man replied. 'Can you tell me where Brick Lane is on this map? Because that's where I'm taking my effing tools. This is no good to me.'

In the East End of London, you didn't make jobs like that. You made it from a photograph, well made, and if it didn't quite match the photograph exactly, you made it look good enough.

Anyway, for myself, I found that this wasn't the way I was going to get a living. I had a friend; and when I told him my troubles — getting a job and staying a job — he said, 'I'll speak to my brother; he's the foreman at Yagars at Ponders End'. Yagers were a firm started by a Rumanian. He's dead now, but he had a place in Stoke Newington, on top of Park Cemetery. He progressed and became quite successful, and decided to expand. He got an old munitions factory on the railway at Ponders End, and employed a thousand people there. You couldn't get very much labour locally, so he tried to get cabinet makers from the East End of London to come down. He got a special concession on the railways and they charged us 10d return from Bethnal Green station to Ponders Station.

When I got down there I found that it was a different kind of place than I had ever seen. It was so vast. There was a big machine shop, with big floor benches dotted all round. It was a time when they were making furniture for hotels. You could probably still find that stuff in some hotels, very cheap kind of work. You had to make 25 tables a day. If you didn't make 25 you were outside, you know. You had to finish them. Some were knocking them up, and the others were finishing them, putting the drawers in. It was very cheap material, the kind of wood that had a grit in it, and you'd have to keep on sharpening your plane, it was so hard on material, with an oak drawer front. A very cheap job.

This was the first time I knew what a union was about. I never knew what a union was for, you see. I had to join a union; got to a place in Brick Lane, on top of a fruit shop there, and I joined the local branch at Number 15. They had meetings in a local pub. You paid shop funds: four pence a week; and for that four pence you got a glass of beer as you entered the pub (which was adjoining the station), and went upstairs to a room, taking your beer up with you.

There was a man working next to me who wasn't very well. He was ill, and he should never have been working, but he had to. He was about 40 and to me that was very old (I was only 19, 20). I'd finished my day's work by about five o'clock, and we used to finish at six. So I thought I'd help him out. We were doing the very cheap drawer tables for the hotel, and I said, 'Give us a couple of your tables', and started putting these drawers in for him. The foreman (a bouncy little fellow) came along and said, 'Whose work is that over there?' I said, 'Mine.' 'Why are you doing this? Have you finished?' he said. 'You can't.' And he was very sharp with his tongue, you know. So I said, 'I'm helping this gentleman. He's not very well.'

'Pack up', he said; just like that. I couldn't understand it. I went and saw the man appointed as a steward (who later became a teacher, funnily enough) and I told him. Well, within ten minutes everything had stopped. It took even less than ten minutes. All the machinery had stopped; it went dead quiet, and everybody started walking out the gate. I thought, 'What are they doing out there? They don't even know me. Why should they go and lose time over me?' I just couldn't make it out. It was explained to me then, they didn't stand that sort of thing. If I'd committed a misconduct of some kind, or my work wasn't good enough, that's different, they couldn't do much about that. But for just helping somebody out... It only lasted about an hour, and I was back at work. That made it a very good trade union. I thought, well, the employer hasn't got all the power.

These men could decide whether there was overtime or not. The employer put a notice on the clock, saying there would be voluntary overtime from such and such, and they could only work overtime if there was a certificate from the union saying they could do that, you see.

I stayed there for some time, and I had an illness for a time. I left the trade then for about 18 months and became a salesman up in Birmingham. Somebody got me a job up there. After a time I came back to London and that trade went down the pan. (It was ladies' summer dresses, and you couldn't sell them in April with the weather very much like December). I got a job then as a clock casemaker. This was something I'd never seen before either; we didn't have a clock at home. When you look back you wonder how you used to live; you didn't have a clock at home, you got up without any clock of any kind somehow.

I got a place making these grandfather clocks. I was glad to get that job. The only reason you could get a job there, they paid very badly. We used to get these mantle clocks, they'd come up in a box, you'd have your front and your back, it was all there in a box, and you'd assemble it, and then veneer it round. It was only a shilling an hour then. The work wasn't as hard as cabinet making, and consequently you didn't need a lot of skill to do that job. You just needed to learn how to starve. It was a non-union shop. I tried to make it into a union shop, but one bloke gave me away. He told the employer. You always find that sort of thing. When the war broke out, in 1939, everybody started looking for war work. I went to my union and they sent me to a job at Greene and Vardey's in Essex Road. (They'd never had a Jew working there before.) They even had a licence to work during the war on the Liverpool cathedral, doing the woodwork. They had the most excellent cabinet makers you've ever known. They were real craftsmen. Each one had a couple of boxes of tools that would have cost hundreds of pounds today. Everything was done by hand there. And they were really good chaps. They were getting half a crown an hour.

They were making munitions boxes for the Navy, solid oak heavy boxes. You knocked up the box, put a lid on and a swing handle over it. At that time there was a lot of war work about. Some cabinet makers went and worked as carpenters sent out to camps in the day. Then I heard of a job going, Metropolitan Plywood Company, but this bloke said, 'Why do you want to go? You got a good job here, good conditions'. It was a very old trade union shop. But I said, 'You can't live on this.' Prices were going up; it was becoming difficult to live on a half a crown an hour. But under the Essential Works Order you couldn't get away without the employer and the Ministry of Trade agreeing. Anyway, eventually I got away and went to the Metropolitan Plywood Company, which was off City Road. It was an old building that had been bombed out. What we were making there was interesting. We were making spare parts of petrol tanks which were put under the wings of fighter planes and dropped in the desert when they were exhausted and there was an extra supply of petrol to the plane. They couldn't land anywhere to get a new load of petrol. (They can today — they can be fed in the air, can't they?)

We had a long bench and you had to build up these parts, which were like a huge bullet, with a nose and a tail, and put stringers in — that's long pieces of wood which were inset all the way round, which we'd cover with a skin. They had to be lightweight because they had to be attached underneath the plane. They had to be made of plywood, and each one was tested for a certain amount of pressure when you'd finished. Whenever they were tested lots were rejected. Some people would put the nose on them and there was still air getting in there, and when the pressure went there, the tail or the nose would be knocked off. You had to be accurate in your work.

It finished up that I spent four years there. I became active and made it into a trade union shop, and I was a trade union chairman and secretary. I was happy in there. We spent a lot of time in air raid shelters you know; the bombs were dropping all the time. But we managed to survive. They didn't know how to sack me. First they offered me a job on the Board of Directors. I went home and I told my wife. She was a very active trade unionist. They offered me £15 a week, which in those days was a big sum. She said, 'If you do, I'll leave you. You mustn't take that.' I went back

and told them, and they were a bit surprised. 'Don't you care about your wife and family?' (I had two small kids then). 'Well, will you take a rise?' they said. So I said, 'Yes, if you give the rise to me, you've got to give it to the chap I'm working next to.' They agreed to that. He got it for a few weeks. Then, when they wanted to cut our bonus of 25 per cent, they tried to use me to allow them to cut it off. When I refused, they cut his bonus and took my bonus away.

There was a lot of machinery there, and a lot of people suffering with dermatitis, caused by a glue called 'Catacolt' glue, made up with a hardener. If you dropped it on your shirt, a drop, it made a hole in it. The reason they had this glue was to withstand the desert heat. They had to withstand all kinds of temperatures. There was a woman there who used to mix it up in a room. You used to have to do a lot of banging, and you got it on your skin. When we were working on time work, it was okay, they used to give you a barrier cream to run into your hands, and if you got anything on your hands, you had to go and wash it immediately. But then they put us on piece work. Now instead of earning say £10, £20 a week, you could earn £30 or £40. Of course people got careless. They saw big money which they'd never known before. The firm didn't care how much they paid. It was a cost plus, you see, whatever the job cost. So I took part in lot of cases at the High Court. The union used to fight these cases for people. Some died from it, they got it so bad. I got a dose that I had to have ten weeks out with it all over my hands.

George Wood,
cabinet maker and turner, b1903

George Wood was born in Gossett Street Bethnal Green in 1903 the eldest of four. His father worked as a cabinet maker and turner and his mother looked after the business. His two younger brothers also went into the trade later setting up as Wood of Ware. George still works most mornings of the week doing turning at a small factory in Hackney that makes reproduction furniture.

My father's place was in Bacon Street. The building is still there now: 60 Bacon Street (a timber merchant that was in Brick Lane took it over). He used to do all the carving work on the articles, on tables and all that. He was also a turner because in those days you had to be everything. You had to be a kind of machinist — there wasn't machines what there are now so you had to do everything. That's how people survived years ago. My father had a circular and chain saw, planer and sander and three turning lathes. The turning lathes were driven by a gas engine from downstairs. The place was owned by a man called Ives, who lived at Romford Road and was a councillor on Bethnal Green. He used to have a wide main belt and shafting running right across the the shops. Two floors and they was all pulleys. If you wanted to let it he'd let you have a path big enough for a wood turner for 5s 6d a week. You made your own belt to run from the counter shaft to your lathe. There were lots of machinists there at that time like fret-cutters, band sawyers, spindlers and spindle moulders. It was all done for the little makers what had shops thereabouts.

I used to take him his dinner when I was about 11 straight from school; and when I was 14 (in 1917) I started working for him as a turner. In those days you worked from eight o'clock in the morning till seven o'clock at night and Saturdays till about two o'clock. And no messing about. When the engine blew up we always sat and worked doing what we used to do when we had no machines. Never stopped still.

When I was 18 I left him and bought my own lathe. I had been earning £3 a week; but you don't ask your father for a rise. I hadn't been an apprentice. The apprentice game was the biggest take-on because you work for so many years for nothing.

I bought this turning lathe and started on my own mak-ing electric floor standards. I was doing pretty good. I did a lot for Beautility. I think they've closed now. Their name was Sadovsky and they let me have a big part of their shop and I employed three, four turners at a time — I went in for all turning. We used any timber, mahogany, walnut, beech, deal, whatever Beautility asked for. When they moved from Hackney Road to Edmonton they left me right in the lurch. Mr Sadovsky said to me, 'Never work for one guvnor' and I never have. I was always interested in furniture, and cabinet work, so I used to go round of a night time and watch this bloke. He taught me how to do cabinet making. He said, 'Do you want to work and learn the trade?' I said, 'Yeah.' 'Well', he said, 'I can give you the same wage as anybody else and as you go on you will get more money.' Of course that is the tale, but it was right with this fella because he was a decent fella. I learnt how to do veneering. It was all done by hand, not on machinery. Soon I had five blokes making real class Regency furniture — not the rubbish called reproduction. We made corner cabinets, Welsh dressers, sideboards, dining tables, Georgian tables. Always in oak. We sold a lot of it down Curtain Road. There were buyers mostly from the East End of London. A little man might make an odd job, take it up there and take it in a shop. But it had to be the goods. It had to be furniture not rubbish like they do now. I used to have a fella come from the West End, Crawford Street. He had an antique business there. His name was Arthur Brother. He'd come down in a van and say, 'I'll have that and that'. Then he'd say, 'I'll see you next week, 'cos I'm bound to sell some of this stuff'.

I was making anything that people wanted. I sometimes got my patterns from a catalogue. I used to say, 'Well, I'll alter that slightly'. But you must keep to the original all the time because they know exactly what they want. I had another bloke from Newcastle upon Tyne. He used to come down himself, the governor. He used to order and said he'd be down in six weeks and take them away. He was the only bloke I knew that gave me the money first.

At that time of day there were timber yards all over the place. Take it from Shoreditch Church. You had Mallinson's, you had two up where the old Penny Bank used to be and one further up on the corner of Temple Street and that was only in one road. They was all round the back turnings. Little yards would go and buy job-lots up and sell it to the makers. According to what kind of wood you wanted you would spend a couple of hours walking round them all. If they haven't got it in that one you'd go to the next one. The big firms such as what used to be Mallinson's and Latham's, they used to supply all the schools for woodwork classes, and of course they had the cream.

When I started as a turner I had a gouge, chisels, flat chisels and plane irons — that's all for top work, which is wide. That's all; and the other one was a machine, a turning machine. We used to get these from Dawes in Bethnal Green Road. Still there — he's not there now,

the grandfather.

In the 1930s my younger brothers still worked for my father. One day I was in Madison Street talking to somebody and I see them coming along on a motor-bike with a carrier on the back behind. The two of them. I said, 'That's funny, they never had that when I was there'. So of course eventually, I found out that they'd both left the old man: left him on his own and started on their own in French Place, Kingsland Road. They started serving my customers; so I didn't say nothing. I thought, 'Oh well, what can you do?' as I was alright with this firm as well. But they started fetching coffee tables etc. and all that, and I never saw them no more after that.

George Wood 1986
(David Dilley)

Sissy Lewis's parents c.1914

Sissy's mother, Beatrice Bentley, who lived in Enfield, worked as a polisher at

Lebus's

(Sissy Lewis)

Sissy Lewis,
sprayer, b1914

Sissy Lewis was born in Tottenham in 1914. Both her parents worked for Lebus; her father as a labourer, her mother as a polisher. In 1928 Sissy followed her parents into the firm where she stayed until the firm closed in 1970.

When I first went to Lebus' I was a sort of sweeper up. I'd clear up in the spray booths. In those days they'd spray one piece of furniture at a time on a turntable. But then, I expect by my mother's influence, I got a job on the new run-way. A run-way is a moving belt where the furniture comes to you, you spray it, then it went away from you. I was fifteen when I first started to spray. Somebody showed me how to do it and the very first bed I was put on, Mr Solly Lebus came and stood behind me. I was scared and couldn't pull the trigger. I didn't get any practice. I went straight onto beds — it didn't matter much about beds, especially the back of them. It was easy to learn and I got into it very well. I worked alongside girls of my own age and some a little older. The older ones were professionals as they had been spraying in the booths. There were no men sprayers at that time. All women and very friendly. We began at eight o'clock in the morning till six at night, with ten minutes for tea. We had a canteen upstairs, one side for staff and one side for the workers. There were no holidays, other than one day in August, Good Friday and Easter Monday. If you were ill you were ill.

The makers used to make all their articles on a bench, then put them onto a moving belt that went onto a big wide moving belt. From this belt they were sorted onto smaller belts that came through our shop. The two spraying rooms were huge with different moving lines for beds, chests, chairs, wardrobes and tables. They were positioned on the belt about two feet apart in such a way that you could spray the sides, the front, the top but not the bottom or the back. You couldn't stop because you were on piecework. If you wanted to go to the lavatory you could miss a turn. As you worked with five other girls every fifth one was yours and if you missed it they got paid for it. Each wardrobe, for instance, had a ticket on it and when you'd sprayed it you took part of the ticket off and at the end of the day you'd give it to the foreman. The polishers

had the same system. But later on we worked as a gang, so whatever we took was divided between the five of us which we found was a a lot better. We were all equal and we had a woman charge-hand for two lines. It stopped all the aggravation. At that time there were eleven belts through the two shops with five sprayers on each.

We didn't maintain our equipment; that was done by a 'gun-boy', a young man about eighteen. He used to come round and do our guns and wash them out. The material came through pipes and from there was a rubber pipe at the end of which was our gun. If anything went wrong with your equipment there was a button at the end of your line to press and a bell would ring. The 'gun-boy' would come along and do whatever we wanted him to. Sometimes a pipe would burst and you'd have to turn the whole thing off and have a new pipe put on.

The spray never made me feel funny and I never had a cold. When visitors came round they used to put handkerchiefs to their noses 'cos of the smell of cellulose. It smelt like nail varnish. People used to say that we should have milk on a job like this but we never did. We didn't have masks or special clothing either.

The lighting was very good but we didn't like the fluorescent because you could never really tell what your job looked like. We all had to work to a pattern. You held it up to the job to see if you had the right colour, and if it was, you were alright. The night light did put you off a bit, it never looked right. The next morning you'd look at it and say, 'Look at that.'

So the first job was to spray the stain to the colour of the pattern. You had no control over the colour as it was all done special according to the work you were on. The stain dried quickly and then you'd lacquer it. It could be either a shiny or a matt finish. Some pieces of furniture like wardrobes were big to do, so they got the tall girls to do them. How they got me on there I don't know but the better sprayers were put on wardrobes. I was always a wardrobe sprayer.

We used to do a lot of shading. I remember doing a dining room suite for America. All you could see of the colour was just an egg shape in the middle, all the rest was shaded. I had to alter the air in my gun so it spitted

Sissy Lewis dancing with Sol Lebus 1964
Sissy and her family were well known to their employers on account of their
length of service and active involvement with the firm.
(Sissy Lewis)

out little spots so it looked as though it had wood-worm.

If you weren't careful the spray could run if you didn't control your gun. If the air pressure was too high and if you pulled the trigger back too far then you'd get a lot of runs and you'd get told off. This furniture you'd take off the line and it would be taken to a little place where men washed it off with stripper. It was a very nasty job. It would then be put back on the belt and you would have to do it again for nothing. If it was somebody else's fault it would be put on the repair line and res-prayed there by one girl. Sometimes you had argu-ments and you were taken in the office and told off. I think it was mostly on the governor's side, not the worker's. Lebus' didn't get unionised till 1939, and only then so they could get government work.

The first job I did in the war was white wardrobes and cupboards for hospitals in France. It was white enamel inside and out. I got covered like a snowman. Then we went onto tent poles and then telegraph poles. The telegraph poles were done with khaki paint, the tent poles red. Even our hair was red and these poles were ever so long. You had to do them on a rack, turn them and spray them. You had to walk along to spray them 'cos they were so long. Then we went onto ammuni-tion boxes. They were khaki with white letters on the front. Then I went into the dope shop where I spent the rest of the war working from seven in the evening until seven in the morning. My husband worked there too on landing craft next to me but he was on days. We used to pass one another in the street, me going to work and him going home.

In the dope shop you had this material called 'madap' which is linen that you put over the plywood of an air-craft. We worked on the Horsa glider which was very big like an underground tunnel about thirty feet across. You moved it round as you worked. Put your back under it and shift it round. We worked in a gang of six, first the 'madap' and then the dope. Dope was like a reddish paint. Terrible smelling stuff. We used to do four of these fuselages a night, which was marvel-lous really. We were the best gang. They put me in charge.

We also made this framework of a lorry in wood. Just the framework. It was then covered with canvas and I had to spray the windscreen, the radiator, the wheels and the numbers. It was then put on the road so the Germans would bomb that convoy of artificial lorries so the real lorries got through. Then we made petrol tanks of plywood that they used to jettison. Later I worked on the Albermarle airplane where I put on the red, white and blue. The Mosquito was different: we just did the wings, and that was all wood and every

square inch a screw hole.

We had a lot of air raids but we never took cover except when it was overhead; just switched all the lights off. Our house in Enfield got bombed. We had a landmine at the back of us and it knocked all our win-dows out and damaged the roof. But we repaired it.

During the war the money was good but we were still on piecework. We said it was wrong that we should be on piecework because men's lives depended on it. In one case we were putting little portholes in a plane and putting madap round so it made the window squ-arish and some of the girls cut through too much and we had a complaint that we were cutting through the ply. In the end it got sorted out because the union was getting stronger.

After the war I became the only woman shop steward at Lebus'. I spoke at our union conference at East-bourne one year against equal pay for women. At the time it was our union policy because, as I said, by hav-ing equal pay for equal work men liked it because it secured their own jobs. Women on the other hand would find it harder to find a job as people would sooner employ men although I insisted that women were better workers. A woman would have her hus-band and children to look after and could lose time from work whereas a man was alright.

I knew that something was wrong as soon as Sir Her-man Lebus died and the two young boys took over (in the 1960s). This fella came in, I've forgotten his name, but he was given a beautiful house and a snooker table in a beautiful snooker room. They said he had come to try and put the firm back on its feet. We rea-lised that something was wrong. We were asked to pull our socks up or else we'd go under. It was all a ter-rible shock. Oh, it was dreadful, fellas were coming along the line shouting out 'We're finished, we're fin-ished, we're closing down!' We all cried. It was a terr-ible time because we'd spent so many years there. Me right from a young girl and my husband from fourteen — and he was fifty eight. He came home crying saying that he'd never get another job. But he did after a fort-night. We were terribly upset. Never thought it would happen to Lebus'. It was one of the biggest furniture manufacturers in the world; three thousand people worked there.

The shop stewards were called into the office and we were told that we would go in groups according to how long we'd worked there. Those who had worked there least years would go first and then down the line. I was one of the last to go with a number of other girls. The oldest Lebus son had us in his office and said how sorry he was. We all talked about the old times and I told him how my mother had worked there in the 1914 war and I remebered her filling up trucks on the sidings. He cried. He thanked us for all the years that we had worked there. We walked out and went over to the pavilion and had our own little parties. Oh dear, it was sad. Part of my life had gone. Fortunately, we got full pay between January and being made redundant in May; plus I got a thousand pounds.

Sissy Lewis with husband, Tom and daughter, Christine 1954
Sissy and Tom Lewis were the only married couple among the employees to attend Sir Herman Lebus's birthday party at the Connaught Rooms, WC2. All those who had worked more than 21 years for the firm were invited. This photograph appeared in the in-house magazine **The Lebus Log** *in September 1954.*
(Sissy Lewis)

Jock Shanley,
upholster and trade union official, b1902

Jock Shanley was born in Aberdeen in 1902, the fifth of seven children. His father was a wholesale fish merchant, but it was his mother who found him a job as an apprentice upholsterer when he left school. He soon became active in the local branch of the Upholsterers Union and in 1924 the Union gave him a two year scholarship to the Central Labour College in London. For some years he worked as an upholsterer before becoming a full time union official in 1934. In 1937 he became the General Secretary of the Amalgamated Union of Upholsterers until 1948 when he became Assistant General Secretary of the National Union of Furniture Trade Operatives when the unions amalgamated. In 1946 he served on the Board of Trade Working Party on Furniture.

I got to know Herman Lebus and became friendly with him when we were on the Furniture Working Party. In fact he more or less invited me to apply to Lebus' as Labour Relations Manager — he had already asked my General Secretary Alf Tomkins who had said no. I laughed. I said ' Sir Herman, Sir Herman I wouldn't last six months in your factory.' And I wouldn't, because he would be going round the factory, and he would see something and he would go up and correct the man. I once went through his research department with him and everyone was giving him the gen of what they were doing and while they were still groping for the answer he would ponder it and come back with the answer. It was the same on the Furniture Working Party. When we had a good discussion Sir Herman would quietly close his briefcase and say, 'Well, I'm sorry, I've an urgent appointment; I must go now'. He would get the meeting adjourned and come back a day or two later with the answers — a remarkable man, but he killed his family and his staff.

He ruled intellectually; he got the answers; he found all the short cuts. But he was trapped like the others with the belt and shaft. So he had a magnificent machine shop but each machine had to be placed according to the source of power. And so the machine shop could not production-wise be in the right order. So there was lots of toing and froing. But it was a complete machine shop.

But he was committed thoroughly to his system; his whole structure was built on it. The individual powerful electric motor enabled other firms to do the same thing on a smaller scale. But what was clear to me, again by talking to the people concerned, is that when the electric motor was attached to the individual machine something fundamental had changed. Now I estimate that it took from 10 to 15 years for the wholesale furniture trade to realise the significance of that change. Gradually the machines were put in line according to the requirements not of power but of production. But each machine still had one big motor. Now that took away the cabinet maker's arms and shoulders. It took away the graft. The machines were far more accurate. I think an alteration in the bearings was responsible. Bearings make the machine run true and able to run to finer and finer limits. So this was the dawn of machine production.

Now each machine was separate and the craftsman was in front of the machine feeding it. There'd be a labourer behind taking it off and putting it on a trolley and conveying it to the next machine where the machinist took it through the next process. But again the significance was in what didn't exist. The gap between the machines. I saw that happening and would speak to employers about their plans. Gradually they built connections between machine and machine and the electric motor in small form was incorporated in each machine. So each machine could perform a variety of functions. And so what became important was the setting of the machine. The machine set-up became more important than the machine operative because the craftsmen then went to the back end of the machine and took off and tested each part against a measuring jig for accuracy. If it went beyond a certain tolerance of accuracy he would stop the machine. Now the skilled craftsmen had gone from the front of the machine feeding it to the back ensuring that it was accurate. This wasn't realised by the trade unions at all. Lebus were important in this process; they had to dismantle their plants.

When I was on the Furniture Training Board I took one of the Directors round a factory, Austin's I think, and I said to him, 'You're going to to speak to a man you won't understand, but listen'. Well, the manager was an old East Ender. He had what the college trained operative didn't have — instinct, in-bred. This Director of the Training Board was bewildered. I said, 'Look, he's a traditional type, but without him there would have been no transition'. But it took a long time for people to realise the difference between machine assisted production and machine production.

Now in upholstery it was different. Round about the 1890s the Cabinet Makers Union took a decision to abolish piece work. Because of the tradition of the garret master sweating the few labourers piece work under handicraft production is exploitation. Piece work under machine production was the next stage of wage development.

But the upholsterer never had the same tradition. Before I came to London from Aberdeen to work in 1926 we still put the webs on by hand, we still sewed the springs to the webs by hand, and we still sewed the springs to the canvas by hand, then a big pile of flock on top and a piece of cotton felt on top of that and you had literally to pull your cover over it. At first in London I was a bit bewildered for instead of stitching a roll, frames were made in the shape the arm would take. You would fix a sausage roll round the woodwork by backtacking a strip of canvas, putting some material in and working it with your fingers so you made a firm sausage. Then you brought that over the edge and tacked it down firm along the edge of the seat. That is for a hard-edged seat, not a sprung edge. Same with the arm. The woodwork of the arm was extended to the final shape of the arm. And so this sausage roll was tacked along the edge of the wood and that gave you the finished edge of the arm. If there were springs put in you tacked it down to the woodwork with staples and put the canvas on.

The better firms would do it in two. They would put a first layer of filling material and then put scrim over it and sew and then button it so that you got a firm base. So you had a variety of qualities in upholstery. But all essentially hand made by the individual upholsterer at the bench. But the upholsterers never repudiated piece work; they organised it.

I know from my experience when I became General Secretary of the Union, the piece worker had to have leaders to produce and organise piece work. In fact in many a factory the shop steward ran the production side. And that was the difference between the upholstery craft and the cabinet maker crafts. They were still in the thick of the struggle: fighting for piece work prices not job-time prices. When we got an agreement, which was about 1909, piece work and piece work earnings were recognised. Piece work jobs had to give an average of x per cent above the timework rate. And when we negotiated an increase in the time work rate we negotiated an equivalent percentage increase in the piece work logbooks.

So our union dealt with all sections and in one negotiation. There would be the most elaborate logbooks maintained, with close job description and a price. It never went as far as the clothing trade or the textile trade, where they still went back to the original price years beyond, plus, minus, and plus minus. Our system in upholstery meant there were people who were alert to every change and so the Upholstery Union built up in a natural way shop leadership. It gave backbone to our union. The cabinet makers still refuse to recognise piece work.

But then changes began. There would be patent springing so instead of webbing putting in individual springs you got a sort of cage of springs. They were fixed by bending the iron bands over the frame and nailing it to the frame and then going to the other end and pulling the band tight and nailing it to the frame. That was labourer's work. There was patent springs for the seat and for the back. Now you can have a new sprung edge because you had your frame of springs with a wire edge. When you pulled the canvas over it you had a moving edge to your back and your seat and you had a moving front to your seat. But they did a strange thing they still used to make a gutter which the old upholsterer used to make between the main seat and the sprung edge. They pulled the gutter of the canvas down and tied it so it gave theoretically free movement at the edge. In fact when you put the cover on you stopped all free movement but we still did it.

Most upholstery remained untouched by machinery apart from that. No machines came into the upholstery shop. Still the pair of trestles and a bench, needles, twine, tacks and a traditional upholsterer's hammer. When you were working with tacks you had a tack-bag and usually half-inch tacks. You'd put your hand in your tack-bag, blow the dust off and into your mouth. You brought the tacks one by one between your teeth with your tongue where you pulled them out. When it came to lunch time or a teabreak, if you still had some tacks in your mouth you just spat them out on the floor. I must have thrown away hundreds of pounds worth of tacks at today's value.

Some years later I was speaking at our East End branch telling them what I thought of the furniture industry. I left them stone silent. An organiser stood up and said, 'There'll never be anything to replace the upholsterer working on a pair of trestles with a mouthful of tacks.' Those are his exact words. I said 'Famous last words.' The stapler and foam were just round the corner.

I ran a campaign for years against foam. We'd lost twenty members in a Glasgow fire. They were trapped in a factory with bars in the windows. In the year of my retirement, 1972, the union journal won a safety award from the Safety Council for its campaign. I ran a campaign to end the menace of foam. The first regulation was to limit the amount of foam in a factory. But the danger was in the home and still is. In the end we got, after I retired, feeble legislation. A little label, rubbish.

Jock Shanley 1950s
At a May Day demonstration in Hyde Park with Ben Reubner, Vic Berlin and Mrs Berlin.
(FTAT)

Henry Doncaster,
polisher b1936

Henry Doncaster was born in 1936 and grew up in Shoreditch and Finsbury where his father was an outside polisher. Henry left school at fourteen and went into polishing where, with a few breaks as a cab driver and motor mechanic, he has been ever since. He presently works as a piece-master in a small factory off the Kingsland Road. One of his early jobs was bleaching an old mahogany sideboard, something many people asked polishers to do after the war when new furniture was scarce.

You strip the sideboard down of all its architectural ironmongery. Then you apply a coat of polish remover — paint stripper — which you lightly scrape off with a steel scraper. This takes off the top surface and then you apply another coat of stripper which you take off with a number 3, 4, or 5 wire wool. These coarse grades of wire wool pull the polish out of the grain. When you've got it clean you wash it down with a mild solution of soda water that has the effect of darkening the wood as well as removing any residues of polish. Then you wired it dry.

Next comes the A and B bleach. It's important to apply bleach from the bottom up so as to avoid runs that would show at the end. The A bleach goes on first all over and is wiped off. Then comes the B bleach. The first coat of B will bubble up mainly because there is some dirt still in the grain. After you've bleached with your B it pays to wipe it down and then apply another thin coat of B. When it looks clean it must be wiped dry and then left for twenty-four hours. If you're happy with the result and its the correct colour it has to be washed down with borax solution which acts as a neutraliser. It's also advisable to wash it down further with acidic acid and finally with clean water. Ideally you should now leave it for a week during which time any remaining bleach in the job will blow out and totally evaporate. The longer you can leave it before rubbing down, coating and fadding up the better.

Fadding up is a way of applying polish by hand. You first coat the area with a brush, a mop — they're special polish brushes. Now you can't keep putting it on with a mop because it's too heavy. The polish goes too thick and you're looking for a nice thin finish. So a fad is similar to an upholsterer's wadding which has been used time and time again as a polish rubber and become hard and very stringy. That makes an ideal fad. After you've applied the polish to the fad you knock it out on a piece of paper to flatten it a little bit. Then with a little bit of linseed oil on the job you start working the polish in and on the job with the fad. You must keep on the move. It's a great job when you're cold. If you dare stop it will stay and become part of the job. It won't want to let go so you must keep it moving. Its a case of working fast and efficiently, keeping the amount of oil down to a minimum and getting into the corners. This builds up the groundwork very very quickly and gives you a nice firm base to work on. It's clean, the grain is filling up and you're doing a good preparation ready for finishing. After leaving to dry over night it has to be cut down with flour paper, that's 400 paper or even finer. Sprinkle a drop of oil on it and away you go cutting it down. It goes really smooth — babies bums don't come into it. Wiping down with a rag comes next. Good cotton curtain is best as it must be lint-free.

Right now you come onto your finishing using a polisher's rubber. A polisher's rubber is made by folding a piece of upholsterer's wadding into a cone shape. It's rather like looking at a funnel but with a nice shape going round. Now you must use cotton for the surface that's not too thin. Bed sheeting is ideal for it needs to have a little body left in it.

Now the polish is applied to the rubber which is then folded over in a particular way and then pressed down so as to distribute the polish evenly. Then you put the cotton over it and draw it across a piece of old sandpaper to take any starch or sheen off.

Applying the rubber to the job is like fadding up; you mustn't stop. If you stop you go straight to gaol. I mean you've blown it. You've got to keep on the move all the time working from the edges inwards. There's an old saying in polishing — well I was told it — take care of the edges and the centre takes care of itself. Now you can use the cross method, go round and round or up and down but you must keep moving now and again applying a spot of oil which can be white oil or linseed whatever takes your fancy. On bleach jobs you must use white oil but most times you use linseed oil. You apply just enough oil to keep the rubber moving nice and free and smooth. Put on the polish from time to time when you feel the rubber drying out too much but keeping your eye on that oil because if you're not careful you end up burying the oil under the polish. That can look good when you're done but within a year or two faint hairline cracks begin to appear. Now if anyone's got that on their old furniture today then that's because oil has been left on the job so it's important to pull that oil out. That's done by gradually decreasing the amount of oil you use and keeping working your rubber and then finally adding a few drops of methylated spirits. Adding spirits does two things. One it pulls the oil from beneath the polish and secondly it thins the polish just very slightly enough to give you a nice bright finish. If you've done the job properly the gloss will finally become enhanced. Any lines will disappear and the whole thing will take on the appearance of a sheet of glass.

If you had to colour up the job you'd do that before fadding up. The whole job would be put together and all the pieces matched up. If it's a light coloured job you would use ochres, the titanium white and flake white. All the mild colours. A little spot of yellow here and there or a spot of red lead or red ochre. Colours to match and to bring things forward very slightly. Not too much or they look too fakey. If you're on darker woods then obviously you go to Venetian reds, brown umbers, blacks and spirit reds. Then you might go into a whole realm of other colours like the analine dyes; the greens, mauves, purples, blues and yellows. There's a whole range of these things that people just don't use today.

If a guy who's done the veneering on a panel has matched his veneers badly you have to stand there and fake the flare and the movement of the timber to match it. There are lots of pieces of furniture today have been done like this and really look the business. But once they're stripped you realise how badly they've been veneered. After the war when materials were scarce people used anything. There are lots of bits of furniture floating around England that if you took the veneer off you would have a genuine Billingsgate box — in fact any box, even orange boxes. You just could not purchase timber so you used anything that was available and believe me around Brick Lane and Spitalfields these materials were generally used.

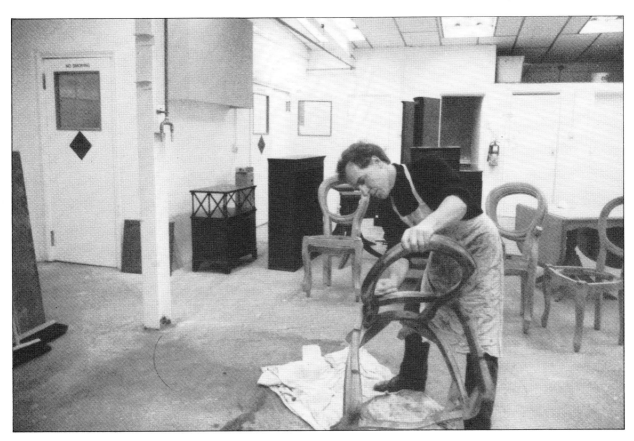

Henry Doncaster 1987
Super-bleaching chair frames at Vinyl Phase Polishers' Tottenham unit for
Dennis Evans of Lewisham.
(Henry Doncaster)

Nathan Rosenberg, cabinet maker, b1908

Nathan Rosenberg was born in Kensal Rise, north west London in 1908, the fourth of seven brothers and one sister. His parents fled the pogroms in Poland arriving in Britain in 1900. He started his working life at thirteen, alongside his father in the family furniture business on Stepney Green. He is still working today.

I designed all my own furniture. Once you know your trade you sketch all the time. I was the worst sketcher in the world but good enough to convey it to my designer. He was very clever at it. Exceptionally clever. When I lost him I lost quite an important person. Ideas generally came from the trade. I used to look around and say, 'I'll make a design or a bedroom suite.' Well, certain articles go on a bedroom suite and I just put them on paper and make a little innovation of my own. Shaping and all that. You see shaped up wardrobes. I think my late father give me the idea of that.

Customers gave me ideas. They'd say, 'I like so and so'. I'd go home and sketch it from the conversation and submit it to them. They'd make their variations and on that I'd take it to my designer and he'd reset it up. My sketch was as good as he'd design, barring he'd make it much better. Make the appearance better to the customer. Sometimes the customer would show you booklets. There wasn't a lot then. Or they'd tell me to go down to a certain store and can I have a look at this. I couldn't stand in the store drawing; you'd get ten years in prison. So you went down, had some ideas and went back. I had it in my mind and sketched it. It wasn't difficult. If you know a piece of furniture, you look at it and say 'It's like that', and that's enough. I could still look at the furniture, go home and sketch it in five minutes. Then again we'd make little alterations to fit in with what they wanted. As to price that's a matter of juggling. I used to work it out to a certain extent.

I'll show you one of my designs I made in the Hackney Road between 1958 and 1965. It's a five foot six sideboard and a five foot serving table. The height is thirty six inches with a three inch pelmet at the back. I'll describe it in the proper cabinet making way.

The doors were coopered up on a pattern, like a frame. Strips of mahogany all planed so you angle them all in one piece. This piece had to have an angle then there was an angle there to make this piece marry to make this shape. Then we used to put on this pattern and then work every piece until it fitted the shape — half a kidney and then a full kidney. Coopering up two doors at that time would take about a day and a half. Then you had to cross veneer them with mahogany, back and front to cover up the joints. You never veneered with the grain, never in cabinet making. With solid you can take a chance. You must go against the grain first then put it with the grain to counter the movement of the wood. You had to four times veneer it mainly to cover up the joints. That means back and front, across, and then along the grain back and front; that made the finish. Then the drawer would go in, coopered in strips. You'd have a width of wood, whatever the drawer was. This one would be about five and a half and six and a half. Eighteen and eighteen equally proportioned. Seven and eight and a quarter, they were the two sizes. You coopered up drawers in wider strips than doors, glued them together and left enough there so that you'd take the backing piece. Then you cut the drawers in. Glued and clamped it. At that time remember we only had scotch glues. With planing and levelling it, it would take three or four hours' work.

Then you'd make the carcase. You've got to cut the rails, the bottom one first. The front which is a wide rail and the back one is a straight rail. Doesn't have to be two and a half inches. The front one has to be about six inches so when you shape up you've got plenty there. Then you put the bottom on next. The top you leave to the end because you've got to shape and then mark from that otherwise you'd have the top one shape and the carcase another.

With the legs that's where the band-saw comes in. You get a three by three square, i.e. that one would be a sixteen or seventeen and a quarter long mahogany. Mahogany was the best wood. Solid walnut was so hard to get hold of and the only walnut you could get in my time was African. We used it and it was quite reasonable but mahogany was always the best one. It was a good wearing wood. Hasn't got a lot of figure in it and you don't get a lot of problems. A lot of good woods like rosewood are so figured that you can never put them with central heating, they change shape altogether. Mahogany didn't do that.

So when you'd cut the leg out to a basic shape you'd give it to the carver. There were many in the Hoxton area, all around there. I'd tell him I want a paw foot and describe the leaf. We usually left the leaf work to the carver himself, 'cos they had patterns. The bottom carving, this was special pierced cut-through carving. All holes and scrolls. I'd cut that out.

Then we'd fit the whole thing together, the two ends, the framing for the doors and two rails — that's a carcase. Tops are all additions. Once you did that then you had to shape. All this had to be levelled down. Then you'd fit your doors, then you'd got the complete shape. Doors and drawer fronts solid. Fit your doors and drawers and they all had to be relevelled. Shaping and all that would be a few days' work. Shaping by hand is a lot of work 'cos you have to be precise.

Once you've got your carcase set up you've got the shape for your top and you always allowed an overlap about five eighths of an inch. All period work of that description overlapped. The top at that time was made of solid mahogany. Later on you made ply. Chipboard isn't bad providing you keep it for tops. Long as you don't screw on it.

The pediment was solid mahogany, veneered to the same burr, then cut to shape. The carver used to carve the centre motif. When you got the carving back you'd assemble the underframe and set your carcase on it. The underframe you tongued and grooved. Tongued and grooved the legs in; it ended up afterwards with dowelling but it wasn't as effective as tonguing and grooving for a dowel could shrink. Tonguing and grooving wouldn't 'cos you made it like a mortice. They don't pull out.

Then you put it together and set it again, reshape it a bit. You had to do that because you had a solid top. Then you'd put the carcase on the underframe and legs and then block it. You'd make one, two, three, four blocks and set them in the corners. You bevelled the blocks off so as they would slide in when you dropped the top on. No glue.

When making the drawers you've got rails set up in the frame. These are chopped in with a shape so they can't pull out. Now you've got to build up your drawers. You fit the two drawers separately into the frame by shaping and planing so every surface goes in perfectly. You've got to put a little bit of an angle on. The back is bigger than the front. When you put it in, especially with shape, your back hits first and your front will come on after and it will fit to perfection. Then you start making your drawers. You have got to make the whole drawer, the two sides, the drawer back and the drawer bottom out of half-inch solid. Clean it all off and then dovetail the lot.

Then the runners go in, two blocks actually. They would rest on the bottom to run on but they're not guiders. When you put a drawer in, it will shake so you put in guiders; they're only thin pieces of wood about three eighths of an inch. You put the guiders just out of square a bit wider to the back. The drawer must be square. Never start messing about with planing drawers, that's a big job, that is.

Now the whole thing is assembled in the white, and doors have to be butted out. Butts being hinges. Then you'd fit the locks and put all the carving on. When its all done you disassemble it, take all the fittings off — not take it to pieces; take the doors off, take all the hinges so they don't get dirty from polishing and give it all to the polisher. There's two sections, that's why I never screwed it down. Just dropped it down. Altogether it would take about three weeks to get to the polishing stage, especially if it was a shaped one.

The polisher would stain it up and leave it over night. Then he'd fill the grain with a similar colour it's got to come out finished. Then they'd start colouring the slightly bad parts of wood which you always have and then papering down after — whether it's staining or filling you had to paper it down. The whole idea of polishing is to have a smooth underneath — polishing's like that. Then we'd bring it back to the shop and fit the handles the customer had chosen. Every customer had their own handles. That was the type of work we did, individual work.

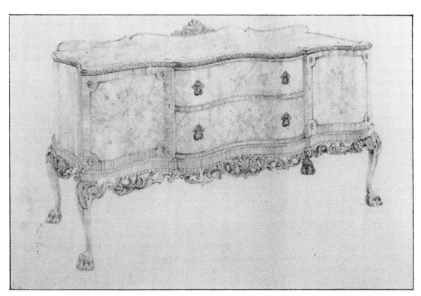

Sideboard c.1960
Designed by Nathan Rosenberg in Hackney Road
'somewhere between 1958 and 1965'.
(Photo Studios)

GLOSSARY

Cabinet Maker

A skilled furniture maker, working in wood. Whereas a joiner is concerned mainly with constructional or fitted woodwork, a cabinet maker specialises in moveable carcase furniture and usually works with a wider range of **solid woods** and **veneers**. Several specialisms (eg fancy cabinet making, table making) exist within the cabinet maker's work. The term does not, however, cover certain branches of the furniture making trade, such as **upholstery**, chair making, polishing, carving or gilding.

Carcase

The frame, or main structure, of a piece of furniture.

Chair Stuffer

An **upholsterer** specialising in stuffing, as opposed to covering, seat furniture.

China Cabinet

A cabinet, usually with glazed doors, made to display china and ornaments. China cabinets were particlarly popular in the 1920s and 1930s.

Chintz

A fast-printed, patterned cotton fabric, usually glazed.

Chipboard

Thin board made of compressed wood chips and resin.

Chisel

A tool which has a steel blade with a square bevelled end, used for cutting and shaping wood.

Cooper Up

To make up parts or pieces of furniture, usually shaped sections, in a similar way to that in which a cooper makes a barrel; thin strips or planks of wood are set vertically into a curved frame, and then shaped to form a smooth curve.

Dovetail

One of the strongest methods of jointing one piece of wood to another, either at right angles or end to end. Rows of fan-shaped **mortices** and **tenons** are cut in each piece so that they slot together. Dovetailing is widely used in the making of boxes and drawers.

Duchesse Table

A type of dressing table popular around the turn of the 19th century, especially among working class newly-weds.

Fitter Up

A **cabinet maker** specialising in making the drawers or compartments within cabinets or boxes.

French Polish

A type of polish made from **shellac**.

Garret Master or Small Master

A furniture maker whose workshop was in his own home or back yard.

Gipsy Table

A cheap, light, round-topped table on three crossed legs; common in 19th century working class homes.

Gouge

A concave-bladed **chisel**.

Greener

An immigrant worker.

Holland

A smooth, hard-wearing linen fabric.

Inlay

A method of decorating furniture by insetting or embedding differently coloured woods, or other material, such as wax, so that they are flush with the surface.

In the White

The state of furniture before it is stained, polished or upholstered.

Japanning

A method of imitating oriental lacquer work by giving wooden furniture a black stain or varnish.

Joint

The point at which two parts of a piece of furniture are joined together.

Journeyman
A skilled worker hired on a temporary basis.

Knock-down
A type of self-assembly furniture sold packed in prefabricated parts, usually with instructions.

Lacquer
A protective, waterproof varnish. It can be made of **shellac** or have a synthetic base, and can be coloured or left clear.

Lathe
A tool or machine for shaping wood. It works by rotating the wood at variable speed, allowing the operator, or **turner**, to shape and decorate it by carving and chiselling.

Learner or Improver
An unofficial apprentice, paid a small wage.

Manufactory
The place where a product is made, usually on a large scale; a factory.

Middleman
A trader — a wholesaler or retailer — who handles a commodity between its producer and its consumer. By taking his 'cut', he forces up its eventual price.

Mortice
Hole or cavity in a piece of wood, cut to receive a **tenon** or projection, on another piece of wood, to form an interlocking joint.

Overmantel
A unit of ornamental shelves, sometimes incorporating mirrors, which is fixed above a mantelpiece. Overmantels were particularly popular in the late 19th century.

Plane
A tool with a wooden or metal stick and a steel blade, used for smoothing the surface of a piece of wood by paring shavings from it. Different grades of plane are used for preliminary shaping, for more accurate fitting and for smooth finishing.

Plywood
Strong, thin board, made from three or more layers of wood glued together with the grain running crosswise.

Scamping
Making poor quality goods.

Scrim
Open-weave fabric, usually cotton, used for lining and **upholstery**.

Shellac
A type of varnish made from the secretion of the lac insect, which is processed by extraction and evaporation into thin sheets. These can then be dissolved in alcohol to form a liquid varnish or **lacquer**.

Slaughterhouse or Slaughterer
A commercial, usually non-manufacturing, warehouse or shop, ordering or buying furniture from its makers at exploitative rates.

Slop
Work done by an exploited or **sweated** labour force.

Solid Wood
A description applied to furniture made entirely without the use of **veneers**.

Sweating or Sweated Labour
A system of sub-contracting, which generates profits for a **middleman**, by 'squeezing' his sub-contractors and forcing them into competition with each other.

Tallboy
A tall bedroom cupboard, with drawers in the upper section.

Tenon
Projection, or tongue, on the end of a piece of wood, which is cut to slot into a corresponding **mortice**, or hole, in another piece of wood, in order to form an interlocking **joint**.

Turning
A method of carving wood on a **lathe**, often used for making the legs of chairs or tables.

Upholstery
The technique of padding furniture — usually seat furniture — with fixed, rather than loose, cushioning material. The padding can be fixed onto a hard foundation, onto interwoven straps of **webbing** or onto canvas, and can be supported by springs. Much modern furniture is padded using synthetic materials, such as foam rubber.

Veneer
A very thin sheet of fine or decorative wood glued to the surface of furniture made of coarser wood.

Webs or Webbing
Traditionally a strong, closely woven cotton fabric, bands of which are interwoven in a criss-cross to form the support for **upholstery** particularly that of chair seats. Nowadays rubber and synthetic materials are commonly used.

BIBLIOGRAPHY

Agius, Pauline, **British Furniture 1880-1915**, Chapter 8, 'The Furniture Trade', (1978)

Amalgamated Union of Upholsterers, **Memoirs of Mr Lewis Leckie, General Secretary 1897-1923. Combining Brief History of the Union**, (1924)

Bale, M.P., **Woodworking Machinery, Its Rise, Progress and Construction**, (1880)

Bevan, G.P. (ed.), **British Manufacturing Industries**, 'Furniture and Woodworking' by J.H.Pollen (1876)

Board of Trade, **Working Party Reports on Furniture**, (1946)

Boone, Gladys, **The Women's Trade Union League in Great Britain and the United States of America**, (1942)

Booth, Charles, **Life and Labour of the People of London**, Vol. IV. 'The Trades of East London Connected with Poverty in the Year 1888', Chapter 6, 'The Furniture Trade' by Ernest Aves, (1893)

Bullock, Amy & Whiteley, Margaret, **Women's Work**, (1894)

Cabinet Maker, The, **Fashionable Furniture. A monthly Budget of Designs and Information for the Cabinet, Upholstery and Decoration Trades**, (1880)

Cabinet Maker, The, **Furniture and Furnishings 1880-1955**, (1955)

Cabinet Maker, The, **Cabinet Maker Directory and Year Book**,(1957)

Cabinet Maker, The, **Cabinet Maker Celebrates a Century 1880-1980**, (1980)

Cohen, B. & Sons Ltd., **A Century of Progress in the Furniture Industry**, (1947)

Drake, Barbara, **Women in Trade Unions**, Chapter 7, 'Wood Working Unions', (reprint 1984)

Falbe, Sophia de, **James Schoolbread & Co. Late Victorian Department Store**, (V&A/RCA Design History Course MA Thesis 1985)

Furniture Industries Research Association, **A Discussion Document on Consumer Attitudes to Buying Furniture**, (1978)

Furniture Industries Research Association, **Buying and Selling Furniture**, (1980)

Furniture Industries Research Association, **Domestic Furniture Purchasing Habits**, (1893)

Furniture, Timber & Allied Trades Union and London Strategic Policies Unit, **Beneath the Veneer, London Furniture Workers Report on the Collapse of their Industry**, (1986)

Goodden, Susanna, **At the Sign of the Four Poster: A History of Heal's** (1984)

Goodman, W.L., **The History of Woodworking Tools**, (1964)

Gossip, Alex, **A History of NAFTA**, (1930)

Greater London Enterprise Board, **Turning the Tables: Towards a Strategy for the London Furniture Industry**, (1985)

Hackney Furnishing Company, **British Homes: Their Making and Furnishing**, (1911)

Hall, P.G., **The Industries of London**, Chapter 5, 'The Older Industries: Furniture', (1962)

Hervé, F., **French Polishers and their Industry**, (1897)

Jeffreys, J.B., **Retailing in Britain 1850-1950**, Chapter 7, 'The Structure of the Furniture Industry', (1977)

Joy, Edward, T., 'The Overseas Trade in Furniture in the Nineteenth Century', **Furniture History**, (1970)

Kirkham, Pat, 'Furniture Makers and Trade Unionism: The Early London Trade Societies', **Furniture History**, (1982)

Kirkham, Pat, **Furniture Making in London 1700-1870: Craft, Design, Business and Labour**, (University of London PhD Thesis 1982)

Latham, Bryan, **Timber: A Historical Survey of its Development and Distribution**, (1957)

Logie, Gordon, **Furniture from Machines**, (1947)

London Cabinets and Upholstery Trades Federation, **London Furniture**, Volume I, (1925), Volume II, (1929)

London School of Economics, **New Survey of London Life and Labour**, Volume II, 'Furnishing and Wood-working Trades', (1931)

Lyall, Sutherland, **Hille — 75 Years of British Furniture**, (1981)

Martin, J.E., **The Location of Industry in Inner North East London**, (University of London Phd Thesis 1961)

Mayhew, Henry, 'Of the Furniture Workers', Letter LXIII, **Morning Chronicle**, (1 August 1850)

Mayhew, Henry, 'Of the Fancy Cabinet Makers', Letter LXIV, **Morning Chronicle**, (8 August 1850)

Mayhew, Henry, 'Of the Slop Cabinet Trade', Letter LXV, **Morning Chronicle**, (15 August 1850)

Mayhew, Henry, 'Of the "Garret Masters" in the Cabinet Trade', Letter LXVI, **Morning Chronicle**, (22 August 1850)

Mayhew, Henry, **London Labour and the London Poor**, Volume II (1861-2)

National Federation of the Furniture Trade, **The Furniture Year Book** (1926)

National Trade Press, **The Furnisher's Encyclopaedia**, (1953)

National Trade Press, **Survey of the British Furnishing Industry**, (1954)

Oliver, J.L., **The Development and Structure of the Furniture Industry**, (1966)

Oliver, J.L., 'In and Out of Curtain Road', **Furniture Record**, (18 December 1959)

Oliver, J.L., 'The East London Furniture Industry', **East London Papers**, Volume IV, (October 1961)

Parliamentary Papers, **Select Committee on the Sweating System** Volume XX, 13, (1888) and Volume XVIII, 5, (1890)

Ransome, Stafford, **Modern Wood-Working Machinery**, (1924)

Reid, Hew, **The Furniture Makers: A History of Trade Unionism in the Furniture Trade 1868-1972**, (1986)

Richards, J., **A Treatise on the Construction and Operation of Woodworking Machines**, (1872)

Salaman, R.A., **Dictionary of Tools used in the Woodworking and Allied Trades c.1700-1970**, (1975)

Samuel, Raphael (ed), **East End Underworld: Chapters in the Life of Arthur Harding**, Chapter 9, 'Cabinet Making', (1981)

Sparks, Penny (ed.), **Did Britain Make It? British Design in Context 1946-86**, 'The Furniture Retailer as Taste Maker', (1986)

Times Furnishing Company, **The Times Furnishing Company: its History, its Service, its Policy**, (c.1925)

Thompson, E.P. and Yeo, Eileen, **The Unknown Mayhew: Selections from the Morning Chronicle 1840-50**, (1971)

Waring and Gillow, **Souvenir Opening of Waring and Gillows New Building**, (1986)

White, Jerry, **Rothschild Buildings: Life in an East End Tenement Block 1887-1920**, (1980)

Wood, A. Dick, **Plywoods of the World, their Development, Manufacture and Application**, (1963)

Periodicals

Cabinet Maker and Art Furnisher

Cabinet Maker and Complete House Furnisher

Cabinet Maker and Retail Furnisher

Furniture Record

NAFTA Monthly Report

NUFTO Record

FTAT Record

INDEX